Helion & Company Limited
Unit 8 Amherst Business Centre
Budbrooke Road
Warwick
CV34 5WE
England
Tel. 01926 499 619
Fax 0121 711 4075
Email: info@helion.co.uk
Website: www.helion.co.uk
Twitter: @helionbooks
Visit our blog http://blog.helion.co.uk/

Published by Helion & Company 2020
Designed and typeset by Farr out
    Publications, Wokingham, Berkshire
Cover designed by Paul Hewitt, Battlefield
    Design (www.battlefield-design.co.uk)
Printed by Henry Ling Limited, Dorchester,
    Dorset

Text © Javier García de Gabiola 2020
Illustrations © as individually credited
Colour profiles © Luca Canossa and
    Anderson Subtil 2020
Maps © Tom Cooper 2020

ISBN 978-1-912866-38-0

British Library Cataloguing-in-Publication
    Data
A catalogue record for this book is available
    from the British Library

We always welcome receiving book
proposals from prospective authors.

CONTENTS

ABBREVIATIONS

AA	anti-aircraft
BC	*Batalhão de Caçadores* (Light Infantry Battalion, literally 'Hunters Battalion')
BCP	*Batalhão de Caçadores* Paulistas (Light Infantry Paulistas Battalion)
BCR	*Batalhão de Caçadores de Reserva* (Light Infantry Reserve Battalion)
BE	*Batalhão de Engheneiros* (Engineers Battalion)
BI	*Batalhão de Infanteria* (Infantry Battalion)
BMCP	*Batalhão de Milicia Civica Paulista* (Civic Militia Paulista)
BRE	*Batalhão Reserva de Engheneiros* (Engineers Reserve Battalion)
CA	*Corpo Auxiliar* (Auxiliary Corps, battalion-sized unit from Rio Grande do Sul)
Capt	Captain (military commissioned officer rank)
Col	Colonel (military commissioned officer rank)
CR	*Corpo de Reserva* (Reserve unit, battalion-type unit from Rio Grande do Sul)
El.	Elements
FP	*Força Publica* (State Military Police or State Militia units)
FPM	*Força Publica Mineira* (Minas Gerais State Military Police)
FPP	*Força Publica Paulista* (São Paulo State Military Police)
GAC	*Grupo Artilleria de Costa* (Coastal Artillery Group)
GAM	*Grupo Artilleria Montada* (Mounted Artillery Group)
GAMtnh	*Grupo Artilleria de Montanha* (Mountain Artillery Group)
GAP	*Grupo Artilleria Pesada* (Heavy Artillery Group)
GIAP	*Grupo Independente Artilleria Pesada* (Independent Heavy Artillery Group)
Gen	General (military commissioned officer rank)
Lt	Lieutenant (military commissioned officer rank)
Lt Col	Lieutenant Colonel (military commissioned officer rank)
1st Lt	First Lieutenant (military commissioned officer rank)
2nd Lt	Second Lieutenant (lowest military commissioned officer rank)
Maj	Major (military commissioned officer rank)
RAM	*Regimento Artilleria Montada* (Mounted Artillery Regiment)
RCD	*Regimento de Cavalleria Divisionaria* (Divisional Cavalry Regiment)
RCI	*Regimento de Cavalleria Independiente* (Independent Cavalry Regiment)
RGS	Rio Grande do Sul
RGN	Rio Grande do Norte
RI	*Regimento de Infantery* (Infantry Regiment)
Sqn	Squadron

1

FROM REPUBLIC TO WAR

Nineteen-thirty-two was the year that the famous Christ the Redeemer was raised on Corcovado in Rio de Janeiro, in front of the Sugarloaf Mountain (*Pâo de Açúcar*), overlooking the beaches of Copacabana and Ipanema.[1] It was the year of the first vibrant Carnival of this beautiful city.[2] It was also the date of the last Brazilian civil war. On 9 July 1932, São Paulo took up arms against the dictatorship of Getúlio Vargas to reinstate the constitution. However, the support promised by the states of Minas Gerais, Rio Grande do Sul and Mato Grosso did not materialise. The Paulistas faced the Federal Army virtually alone and were defeated after almost three months of fighting. Despite being the richest and most advanced state of Brazil, equipping some 35,000 combatants and turning their industry to the service of the war, the Paulistas saw their ammunition run out and were crushed by a mass of 100,000 Federal soldiers (with 60,000 in the front line) who advanced concentrically from all the state borders. Although erroneously labelled as separatists, this was really a war to restore democracy throughout Brazil, where paradoxically, the bourgeois were the rebels and the revolutionaries were the government.

This war will be narrated in two separate volumes. The main front was initially the eastern Paraiba Valley that led to Rio de Janeiro, the then-capital of Brazil. The 2nd Division mutinied and advanced against Rio, but was stopped dead on the frontier between Rio and São Paulo by the loyal 1st Division based there under General Góis Monteiro. After three months of trench warfare between around 20-22,000 Federals and some 8-10,000 rebels, and despite advancing some 70km, the Federals were still some 150km from São Paulo City when the war ended. The rebel forces were nearly surrounded from the south due to the withdrawal of the rebel forces in the Coast Sector. The fighting in these two sectors will be covered in this volume. In the South of São Paulo State, the Federals created the South Detachment, made of the Federal 3rd and 5th Divisions, the 3rd Cavalry Division and the Gaucho Brigade of Rio Grande do Sul, totalling some 18,000 men against just 3-5,000 Paulistas. The Federals broke the front in Itararé on 17 July, producing the largest advance in the war, but they were still very far from São Paulo when the war ended. There

Paulista President Washington Luiz, on the left, talking with Júlio Prestes. (Coleção Verdiana Prado, via Donato)

Views of São Paulo's industrial quarter in the 1920s before the war. (Industrias Reunidas Francisco Matarazzo, via Donato)

President Washington Luiz's face shown in the shape of São Paulo State in a political propaganda cartoon. (Coleção Paulo Florençano, via Donato)

A view of São Paulo in 1930, before the war. (Della Rosa, via Historia y Vida)

was also some fighting in Mato Grosso do Sul following the path of the Parana and Paraguay rivers, in Manaus and Rio Grande do Sul. Finally, the decisive front was the Minas Gerais Front, that was only active since 2 August. The 4th Federal Division based there, with the Police of Minais Gerais and other states' troops, broke the front in Eleutério on 26 August, advancing some 50km to near Campinas, adding 18,000 soldiers against some 7,000 Paulistas. They were just some 70km from São Paulo City, and the Paulistas finally surrendered on 2 October. This set of battles and the end of the war will be narrated in volume two.

To understand the conflict, it is necessary to look back to 1889, when the Emperor of Brazil was deposed by a coup that established a republic. This revolution reconciled the wishes of progressive young officers of the armed forces – who were demanding a modernisation of the country – and of the big landowners – who were protesting against the recent abolition of slavery. However, the middle class was still nearly non-existent, while the mass of former slaves was illiterate although free for the first time in centuries; therefore, neither was present on the political scene. Moreover, except for the reforming governments of the early years, the dominating political class – leaning

upon a system of family clans and the protection of the interests of two major economic and urban centres, São Paulo and Minas Gerais – wielded power and promoted only its own interests, while lulling the population into a relatively dormant state. Correspondingly, no matter that it may have been described otherwise, the actual system of governance in Brazil of the 1930s was not one of political parties, but one of protecting private interests – first and foremost São Paulo's coffee industry and Minas Gerais' lactucarium industry. Unsurprisingly, the politics became known as 'Coffee and Milk' (*café com leite*).[3]

Vargas' Revolution of 1930

The political system collapsed with the revolt in 1930 by Gaúcho lawyer and Rio Grande do Sul politician Getúlio Dorneles Vargas. The fuse was lit when the president of Brazil, Washington Luiz from São Paulo, wanted to skip the turn of the 'milk' and instead repeat the turn of the 'coffee', placing another Paulista in the office. The marginalised landowners and the 'Lieutenants', led by Vargas, disgruntled with the system, took the opportunity to rise – just as they had done at the end of the Empire. Ultimately they triumphed, destroying the First Republic in the process and laying the foundations of the so-called *Estado Novo*

A view of Estação Dom Pedro II, Rio de Janeiro, in November 1930, celebrating Getúlio Vargas's assumption of power. (Arquivo Nosso Século, Revista da Semana, 1930, via Donato)

for his generous and paternalistic social policy, and for improving their rights and working and living conditions, the position of his government was relatively stable. However, because of the absence of political guarantees for freedoms of any kind, the longer he remained in power, the more concerned the emerging middle class became that Vargas's rule might develop into either a communist or fascist dictatorship.[4]

During 1932, São Paulo was a hotbed of political discussion on the new methods of governance, abounding with demonstrations and even several armed clashes between supporters of the different factions. The Constitutionalist Movement,

(New State). Getúlio Vargas, a very intelligent, practical and conniving man, rose to power: in addition to suppressing the political influence of the big landowners, he suspended the constitution, dissolved the federal and state parliaments, and launched political reform through the means of emergency rule. Because the working class adored him contrary to Vargas, intended to reinstate – or at least approve – a new constitution as soon as possible, to restore democracy and protect the rights of citizens with certain guarantees. To calm the boiling atmosphere, Vargas announced elections for May 1933, and his intention to draft and adopt a new constitution. However, it was already too late and before long the streets were out of control. General unrest culminated on 22 May 1932, when a crowd rushed to the Champs Elysees and demanded that the governor of São Paulo, Pedro de Toledo (appointed by Vargas), join the Constitutionalist cause. Overwhelmed and flattered, Toledo switched sides and supported the demands. The same day, several hundred students (their exact number remains unknown) attacked the offices of multiple newspapers that

President Washington Luiz, exiting Copacabana Fort to go into exile after being arrested. (Arquivo Nosso Século, A Noite, rotogavura 26.11.1930, via Donato)

President Getúlio Vargas and future Minister Osvaldo Aranha, on the left, saluting the people gathered outside the Catete Palace in October 1930. (Arquivo Nosso Século, photo by Luís Bueno Filho, via Donato)

A view São Paulo during the 23 May clashes between Varguistas and Constitutionalists that ended in the killing of five teenagers. (Della Rosa, via Historia y Vida)

MMDC Militia poster commemorating the killing of the students in the assault on the pro-government newspaper offices. These were Miragaia, Martins, Darauso and Camargo. (Daróz)

Two views of the people supporting the Constitutionalist movement under the São Paulo flag. From the clothing of the people shown in the photographs, it's clear that the supporters of the revolution were of the middle classes. (Coleção Paulo Florençano, Taubaté, via Donato)

São Paulo governor Pedro de Toledo, saluting after being acclaimed by the people. (A Gaçeta São Paulo, via Donato)

supported Vargas. When the occupants defended themselves, a shootout followed in which at least five Constitutionalist teenagers died. As a result, an illegal paramilitary militia named the MMDC (named for the initials of four of the teenagers killed) came into being and began organising an uprising.[5]

Preparations for the Constitutionalist Revolution

At the same time, Vargas adopted the State Governors Code, a regulation issued to increase the responsibilities of the central government, while reducing those of local governments. While certainly necessary, this aroused much opposition among political elites: this was a traditional political conflict in Brazil, which had already been through two civil wars – in 1893 and 1923 – in the state of Rio Grande do Sul over similar issues. However, while under the old constitution the Federal Army was prohibited from intervening in such cases and – at least in theory – had to observe impassively, regardless of the violence, under the new law the armed forces now had the right to become involved. Misinterpreting Vargas's intentions, the Constitutionalists concluded that he was about to curtail civil rights and saw themselves as having no other option but armed conflict.

The discontent in São Paulo had meanwhile reached senior officers of the Army, who were unhappy with the way Vargas has distributed various of their posts – the primary reason for which was that the president had favoured the *Tenentes* that supported him during the 1930 Revolution. Eventually, the disaffected Army officers established ties with the disaffected civilians, and the two then developed links to the officers of the São Paulo Military Police (*Força Publica de São Paulo*, FPP) – the local armed forces, and the police of São Paulo State. Those involved decided to wait for General Bertoldo Klinger, commander of the 1st Circunscription in Mato Grosso, who was expected to bring 5,000 troops with him on 14 July 1932.

Meanwhile, other anti-Vargas groups began preparing themselves in Minas Gerais, Rio Grande do Sul and Rio de Janeiro.

The overall picture was that – rather paradoxically – the revolutionists were actually conservatives, while the government was the revolutionary force in the following conflict. Moreover, Vargas's government was very lucky that due to several mistakes on the part of Klinger (as will be described later in this work), the perpetrators of the uprising decided to launch their coup five days earlier than originally planned – on 9 July – while the mass of their followers were still not ready.[6]

2
THE BRAZILIAN ARMED FORCES

The War of 1932 – also known as the Paulista War or the Constitutionalist Revolution – involved the central Federal Brazilian Army and the local armies of each state of the Federation, usually called *Força Publica* (FP), or more informally the State Police. These units would be joined by volunteer corps, generally formed in each of the states. Thus, both government forces and rebel units included regular Federal Army, state and voluntary corps.

Clearly, the most powerful, best-armed and best-organised was the Federal Army, established by Decree No. 13,916 of 11 December 1919 and No. 15,235 of 31 December 1921. Under the latter legislation, the Army was to consist of eight divisions, of which five were infantry divisions (designated from 1 to 5) and three cavalry divisions (designated from 1 to 3), while in addition there was a Mixed Brigade. Their geographical distribution is detailed in Table 1.

Generally, Rio Grande do Sul had the highest concentration of armed forces, with the 3rd Infantry Division and the three cavalry divisions. This deployment was quite logical considering that these units guarded the more accessible borders of Brazil with Paraguay, Uruguay and especially Argentina, its historic arch-rivals. Further units were deployed along the coast from south to north, including the 5th Division (Paraná), 2nd Division (São Paulo), 1st Division (Rio de Janeiro) and 4th Division (Minas Gerais). The Mixed Brigade was located in Mato Grosso in the interior, and in the north and north-east of Brazil there were up to 11 independent battalions. Of all these units, only the 2nd Division and half of the Mixed Brigade finally joined the rebellion.[1]

Federal Infantry and Artillery

Each of the infantry divisions of the Brazilian Army in 1932 consisted of three light infantry battalions (*Batalhão de Caçadores*, BC). These were numbered consecutively from 1st to 3rd for 1st Division, from 4th to 6th for 2nd Division, and upwards for remaining divisions. Moreover, each division consisted of three infantry regiments (RIs), designated following the same system, from 1st to 15th. Therefore, 1st, 2nd and 3rd RIs and BCs belonged

Map of Brazil – with the boundaries of federal states as in the present day – showing major unit deployments. Marked in grey are the federal states (São Paulo and the southern part of Mato Grosso called Maracaju, nowadays Mato Grosso do Sul), and military units (foremost 2nd Division and the Mixed Brigade) that rebelled against the federal government. (Map by Tom Cooper)

Table 1: Brazilian Federal Army, Order of Battle, 1932 (Units marked in bold joined the mutiny.)

State/Region	Military Region	Division/ Brigade	Regiments	Other Units	Hq Location
Rio do Janeiro	1st Region	1st Division	1st RI		Villa Militar, Rio
			2nd RI		Villa Militar, Rio
			3rd RI		Praia Vermelha
			1st RAM		Villa Militar, Rio
			2nd RAM		Santa Cruz
			1st RCD		
				1st BC	Nitheroy
				2nd BC	Petropolis
				3rd BC	Villa Militar, Rio
				1st BE	Villa Militar, Rio
				1st GIAP	Cascadura
				1st GAMtnh	Campinho
		Independent	15th RCI		Villa Militar, Rio
		Independent	Naval Fusiliers Regiment		
		Independent		Railroad Battalion	
		Independent		1st GAC	Santa Cruz
São Paulo	**2nd Region**	**2nd Division**	**4th RI**		Quitaúna
			5th RI		Caçapava/ Lorena
			6th RI		São Paulo
			3rd RAM *		Campinas
			4th RAM		Itu
			2nd RCD		Pirassununga
				4th BC	São Paulo
				5th BC	Probably at Piraçicaba
Minas Gerais, or Goias				6th BC**	Uberaba, or Ipamery
São Paulo				**2nd GIAP**	Jundiahy or Quitaúna
				2nd GAMtnh	Jundiahy
				2nd BE	
		Independent		**2nd GAC**	Santos
Rio Grande do Sul	3rd Region	3rd Division	7th RI		Santa Maria
			8th RI		Cruz Alta
			9th RI		Rio Grande
			5th RAM		Santa Maria
			6th RAM		Cruz Alta
			3rd RCD		
				7th BC	Pouso Alegre
				8th BC	São Leopoldo
				9th BC	Caxias
				3th GIAP	Montenegro
				3rd GAMtnh	São Gabriel
				3rd BE	Cacequi
		1st Cavalry Division	1st RCI		Santiago de Boqueirao
			2nd RCI		
			3rd RCI***		
			4th RCI		Santo Angelo

Table 1: Brazilian Federal Army, Order of Battle, 1932 (Units marked in bold joined the mutiny.)					
State/Region	Military Region	Division/ Brigade	Regiments	Other Units	Hq Location
				1st GAM	
				2nd GAM	
		2nd Cavalry Division	5th RCI		
			6th RCI		Alegrete
			7th RCI		
			8th RCI		Quarahim
				3rd GAM****	
		3rd Cavalry Division^	9th RCI		São Gabriel
			12th RCI		Bage
			13th RCI		
			14th RCI		Dom Pedrito
Minas Gerais	4th Region	4th Division	10th RI		Tres Coraçoes
			11th RI		São João de Rei
			12th RI		Belo Horizonte/ Para
			7th RAM		Juiz de Fora
			8th RAM		Pouso Alegre
			4th RCD		Tres Coraçoes
				10th BC	Ouro Preto
				11th BC	Diamantina
				12th BC	Curvello
				4th GIAP	Oliveira
				4th GAMtnh	Pouso Alto
				4th BE	Itajubá
Paraná	5th Region	5th Division	13th RI		Ponta Grossa
			14th RI*		Existed only on paper, pending recruitment and establishment
			15th RI*		Existed only on paper, pending recruitment and establishment
			9th RAM		Curityba
			10th RAM		Rio Negro
			5th RCD		Castro
				13th BC	Joinville
				14th BC	Florianópolis
				15th BC	Curityba
				5th GIAP	Guarapava
				5th BE	Curityba
				5th GAMtnh	Valença
		Independent		3th GAC	Iataipus
Mato Grosso	1st Circunscription	Mixed Brigade	**Mixed Artillery Regiment**		Campo Grande
		Independent		**10th RCI^^**	Bela Vista
		Independent		**11th RCI^^^**	Ponta Porá
				16th BC	Cuyaba
				17th BC	Corumbá
				18th BC	Campo Grande

Table 1: Brazilian Federal Army, Order of Battle, 1932 (Units marked in bold joined the mutiny.)

State/Region	Military Region	Division/ Brigade	Regiments	Other Units	Hq Location
				6th BE	Aquidauana
				5th GAC	Coimbra
North-western Brazil	6th Region			19th BC	Bahia
				20th BC	Maceio (Alagoas)
				21st BC	Recife (Pernambuco)
				22nd BC	Parahyba
				23rd BC	Fortaleza (Ceará)
Northern Brazil	7th Region			24th BC	(São Luiz) Maranhao
				25th BC	Teresina (Piauí)
				26th BC	Belem (Pará)
				27th BC	Manaus (Amazonas)
				4th GAC^^^^	Obidos (Amazonas)

Notes

* Unit existing on paper, but not mentioned in any report during the war.

** Pertaining to the 2nd Division, despite not being based in São Paulo State. Sources differ whether it was based in Minas Gerais or in Goias. The unit remained loyal.

*** Unit existing on paper, pending its recruitment and establishment.

**** Only one artillery group was established.

^ Artillery groups were not established.

^^ Unit neutral initially; by mid-July the unit had split, with half supporting each side.

^^^ Unit initially neutral, then joined the mutiny on 20 July 1932.

^^^^ Unit joined the mutiny on 18 August 1932.

o 1st Division, for example. In turn, each of the RIs was composed of three infantry battalions (BIs), designated I to III, and a company of machine guns. Each battalion was subdivided into three infantry companies and one company of heavy machine guns. The *Caçadores* battalions had the same organisation but their heavy weapons company was armed with a mix of light and heavy machine guns.[2]

Every division of the Brazilian Army included two mounted artillery regiments (RAMs), each of which consisted of two artillery groups. The groups in turn consisted of three batteries of four artillery pieces each. An exception to this rule were the independent groups, which usually had only two artillery batteries. Correspondingly, each group had eight to 12 artillery pieces, and each regiment 24. The RAMs were armed with artillery pieces mounted on carts in order to provide them with improved mobility in the rugged Brazilian terrain. They were designated consecutively from 1st to 10th: 1st and 2nd RAM were assigned to 1st Division, 3rd and 4th to 2nd Division and so on. The artillery component was completed by the heavy artillery group (GIAP) and a mountain artillery group (GAMNHA), designated with the same number as their parent division.[3]

Further support units in every division included an engineer battalion (*Batalhão de Engheneiros*, BE), and a divisional cavalry regiment (RCD). The former nominally consisted of three companies: one of sappers, another of pontoons and the third for communication.[4] The RCD consisted of three squadrons and acted as an advanced guard or for reconnaissance operations. Both the BE and the RCD were always designated as per their parent division (for example, 1st RCD or 1st BE for 1st Division).[5]

However, while the establishment of all of these units was officially sanctioned by 1932, not all were actually established. Indeed, it seems that many existed on paper only, or were of a cadre of officers alone, and were waiting for their turn to be fully manned, equipped, trained and activated.[6]

Cavalry and Independent Units

The three cavalry divisions of the Brazilian Army in 1932 each consisted of four independent cavalry regiments (RCIs), designated consecutively from 1st to 4th for 1st Cavalry Division, and 5th to 8th for 2nd Cavalry Division. The RCIs assigned to 3rd Cavalry Division were an exception in so far as these were designated 9th, 12th, 13th and 14th. Nominally, each cavalry regiment – regardless whether RCD or RCI – consisted of four squadrons of horsemen. Although in theory each should have had two horse artillery groups attached, actually only 1st and 2nd Groups of 1st Cavalry Division and 3rd Group of 2nd Cavalry Division were established. In similar fashion, none of the mounted infantry battalions planned to be established and assigned to each division had been organised as of 1932.[7]

The sole mixed brigade of the Brazilian Army in 1932 was something of an exception. It consisted of three battalions of *Caçadores* (16th, 17th and 18th), two independent regiments of cavalry (10th and 11th), a mixed artillery regiment and one engineer battalion (6th).[8]

In addition to the units integrated into brigades and divisions, there were a number of independent units, such as 19th to 29th *Caçadores* Battalions. All were deployed in the north and north-east of Brazil, while 15th RCI, which had only two cavalry squadrons, was deployed in Rio de Janeiro. Furthermore, there were five artillery coastal groups (GACs, designated consecutively from 1st to 5th), eight independent coastal batteries, the Railroad Battalion (*Ferroviario*) and a tank company. The latter was actually dissolved before the war but was then reorganised as a tank section. Finally, shortly before the war, on 29 February 1932, the Naval Fusiliers Regiment was established for amphibious operations and to garrison naval and riverine bases.[9]

Numbers of Troops Involved

Sources differ, but it is possible to conclude that as of 1932, the total strength of the Brazilian Army was between 53,000 and 62,395 soldiers.[10]

The above-mentioned Decree of 1921 provided authorised strengths for specific units as follows:

- Infantry regiment: 1,309 officers and other ranks;
- *Caçadores* battalion: 477 officers and other ranks;
- Infantry battalion: 436 officers and other ranks;
- Divisional cavalry regiment: 423 officers and other ranks;
- Mounted artillery regiment: 930 officers and other ranks;
- Mixed artillery regiment: 660 officers and other ranks;
- Artillery group: 228–246 officers and other ranks;
- Engineer battalion: 440–465 officers and other ranks.

One exception to this rule was the 1st RCD, which had an authorised strength of 679 officers and other ranks, as per an independent cavalry regiment; another was the 15th RCI, which totalled only 375 troops.[11]

Therefore, if all of its elements were fully staffed, each of the four infantry divisions was supposed to include 8,352 officers and other ranks, while a cavalry division was supposed to include 3,208 men. However, these figures did not include their logistical support units, which is one reason why the actual strength of every division was quite different. For example, on 16 July 1932 1st Infantry Division totalled 9,067 officers and other ranks, while 4th Division had only 4,340 troops. In comparison, 2nd Division – which joined the rebellion – totalled only 3,635 officers and other ranks. Of course, all units – both loyalist and rebels – soon bolstered their strength through activating reservists.[12]

The Força Publica

As mentioned above, both sides included regular troops, but there were also almost as many soldiers from the contingents of the *Força Publica* (FP) of each state. The FP can be understood as a mix of a military police, state police and state militia: it was operational in every state of the Brazilian federation and kept strictly under the control of the local authorities. Little is known about their total strength, but a report for 1926 cited the FP as being authorised to have 39,516 officers and other ranks, but actually totalling 45,821.[13]

While detailed records are not available, it is apparent that in the Paulista-controlled territories, the FP units – and associated militias – provided at least half of the troops that took part in the fighting. The situation was quite similar in the areas controlled by the loyalists: indeed, as an approximation, if we compare the FP numbers of 1926 with the Federal soldiers in 1932, the proportion of officers and other ranks from the FP is about 42 percent of the total force.[14]

As could be expected considering its population and economic might, São Paulo originally had the biggest FP contingent, counting 14,254 officers and other ranks. By 1932, this was decreased by Vargas to about 10,000 – apparently as a punishment for opposing him during the 1930 Revolution.[15] It was for the same reason that the Paulisita State Aviation was dissolved during the same period.

The second-largest FP was that of the Rio Grande do Sul, with 8,597 officers and other ranks – well above the 3,182 that were officially authorised – all organised into the military brigade. Bahia, with an FP of 4,000, was followed by the Federal District of Rio de Janeiro,

and Minas Gerais – the latter with 3,700 troops, somewhat below authorised numbers. Pernambuco had 2,381 officers and other rank in its FP, while the states of Ceará, Piauí and Rio de Janeiro each had about 1,000. All the other federal states combined added up to 5,828 soldiers, fewer than the 6,059 they were authorised.[16]

Regarding the units formed by every state, Rio Grande do Sul sen up to 27 to the Southern Front (for even 50 units in total, depending or the source), mostly from the Provisional Corps (*Corpos Provisorios*) and including several cavalry regiments. Those known to have taken part in the fighting were 2nd and 3rd Cavalry Regiments, 1st, 2nd, 4th 5th, 8th Infantry and 8th Reserve Battalions, and 3rd, 8th and 17th Auxiliary Corps.

Minas Gerais provided another 20 battalions of the FPM designated from 1st to 20th, and organised into North, Centre and South Brigades. Indeed, this state was the only one to group its battalions into large units such as brigades. Paraná deployed at least three battalions of its FP, grouped into one or two 'detachments', while Lima Cavalcanti, in Pernambuco, proposed the establishment of the Division Nordestina of up to 35,000 troops under his command, but Vargas refused. Instead, he accepted the establishment and deployment of small units of around 500 each, that would be sent to the front lines. Finally, the Mineiro Triangle area offered up to 15,000 troops, but never deployed this many.[17]

The other contributions by states were lower, but in no case negligible. From the north and north-east emerged multiple units. Piauí, for example, enrolled 550 soldiers, sent another 407 from the '*João Pessoa*' BC to the Paraíba Valley and requested weapons for 2,000 more. In the end, they formed three battalions of volunteers. Pernambuco promised 6,000 troops, and on 23 July embarked 1st BCFP, organised 2nd BCFP and then proposed to equip between 500 and 2,000 volunteers over the next week. Sergipe sent 28th BC (Regular), but promised to reinforce it with 500 soldiers, and sent the FPS Expeditionary Battalion to Rio de Janeiro. Bahía should have deployed 11th BC, but this remains unconfirmed: it did send 1,200 state troopers and 2,000 fresh recruits though. In mid-July 1932, Ceará sent 23th BC (Regular) with only 342 soldiers, instead of the 800 promised, along with the 1st Provisional Battalion of 572 soldiers, and on 13 September, the 2nd and 3rd Battalions of 525 men each, although the latter ones came too late to fight. Paraíba State forwarded three battalions of the FP: one for Minas and two for the Southern front. Alagoas sent at least the 1st Provisional Battalion of the FPA. Rio Grande do Norte also sent at least one battalion.[18]

A few contingents from central and southern Brazil also appeared on the battlefield. Espirito Santo deployed the 1st Battalion FP with 600 veterans; Santa Catarina sent either one or two battalions to the South (only one was ever mentioned as in action); Goiás deployed a battalion of its FP and reinforced the Ludovico and Rabelo Columns that were operational against the rebels in what is nowadays Mato Grosso do Sul; and Mato Groso probably deployed its two battalions of the FP and two cavalry regiments known to have been established already in 1917.[19]

All Brazil with Vargas

Eventually, forces loyal to Getúlio Vargas thus mobilised all of the resources of the about 30 million inhabitants of Brazil to crush the rebellion. Moreover, the president ordered the fleet to block all of the Paulista-controlled coast – and especially the port of Santos – to prevent the import of equipment purchased abroad by the rebels. Fortunately for the government, practically all of the negotiations that the rebels had with Argentina, Italy, the United States and Paraguay failed, and thus – and with very few exceptions – São Paulo was forced rely on its own resources.[20]

On top of that, Vargas cleverly won the support of the majority of the Brazilian population in selling the idea that the Paulistas wanted independence and to create a pro-Italian republic. Misguiding the public in this regard proved easy because out of about seven million Paulistas, about 50 percent were immigrants, mostly of Italian origin. This – and the defence of the unity of Brazil – became the primary reason why all the federal states rushed to offer their FP units to Vargas's aid. Paradoxically, this misconception about the Paulista independentism can be traced to this day: in large parts of the Brazilian population this war is remembered as a struggle for independence, i.e. one with a separatist agenda.[21]

Eventually, thanks to the contributions of various states, Vargas was able to assemble an army of about 100,000 troops, which was plenty enough – even if a far cry from 300,000–350,000 claimed by some of the Paulista authors. With this, the Federals had an overall numerical superiority of three-to-one against the rebels, even if in practice this was usually reduced to two-to-one on the battlefield as sizeable segments of the armed forces were kept back to control the population and prevent possible additional uprisings.[22]

The Paulista Forces

As of 10 July 1932, the Paulista forces included about 10,000 FP troops, 3,635 officers and other ranks of 2nd Infantry Division (all of which joined the rebellion, except for 6th BC based, depending on the source, either in Uberaba, in the Triangle Mineiro – the Mineiro Salient – or in Goias). Before long, they were reinforced by an unknown number of reservists and about 20,000 volunteers.

Indeed, early on, volunteers flocked en masse to the Paulistas: between 11,000 and 18,000 regular troops and FP soldiers joined the movement: while most of the available sources quote the establishment of 40 volunteer battalions, actually no fewer than 80 of these came into being, each about 200–300 strong.[23] The composition of these units, and their designations, reflected the kind of people who joined the cause. Colonel Taborda, who joined the rebellion, for example, commented that his troops were almost exclusively lawyers and doctors. Most of the units consisted of troops who were friends or relatives, or residents of the same neighbourhood, as in the case of the Battalion of East São Paulo (*Batalhão de Este de São Paulo*). Other units consisted of people from the same factory (Railway Battalion/ *Ferrocarril*), profession (Public Officers/*Batalhão de Funcionarios*, Volunteer Teachers/*Batalhão de Profesores Voluntarios*, and Blacksmiths and Scrap Workers/*Batalhão de Ferragista*) or the same school (*Batalhão de Escola*), the same court (*Batalhão de Jiustiça*) or the same university (*Batalhão de Universidade*), while some – like *Batalhão de Esportivo* – were based on little other than a common hobby (football),

beliefs (*Batalhão de Archidiocesano*) or even colour of the skin (*Legião Negra*).[24]

Of much greater concern to the Paulistas than the number of troops were the number of arms. Although the arsenals of São Paulo should have contained between 15,000 and 29,000 rifles, and there were a further 8,685 rifles from FP stocks, 7,800 rifles from Army stocks, as well as 144 heavy machine guns and 515 sub-machine guns, many of these were either obsolete or in very poor condition.[25] The FP provided about 7,800 additional rifles, but 36 percent of these were hopelessly obsolete Mauser 1895 models that had not been calibrated and were thus extremely inaccurate. Finally, Mato Grosso, which had about 5,000 rifles in its armouries, sent only 80 rifles and 450 obsolete muskets to the Paulistas. Thus, the Paulistas never managed to arm

Four middle-class Paulista volunteers, with their military equipment and uniform, just before departing to the front. Notable is the Paulista white handkerchief of the soldier on the left, and that all four (including the grandfather of the owner of this photograph) are smiling: they were probably a group of friends enrolled in the same battalion, and considered the war to be an adventure. (Della Rosa, via Historia y Vida)

Paulista volunteers departing to the front from Sorocabana Station.
(Waldemar Martins Ferreira Filho, via Donato)

A Paulista *matraca*, a kind of rattle to simulate the noise of a heavy machine gun. (*Diários Associados*, São Paulo)

Paulista propaganda poster for the 'Gold for São Paulo' initiative. (Arquivo Nosso Século, via Donato)

Paulista propaganda posters asking for volunteers to reinforce the MMDC Militia units. (Arquivo Nosso Século, via Donato).

is actually very little in overall context: for an army of 30,000 troops, it means only about 4.4 bullets per soldier per day. Unsurprisingly, General Klinger attempted to acquire 500 million additional cartridges in New York, however, this attempt failed. Thus, much of the fighting ended after only a few hours, simply because the Paulistas ran out of ammunition and were then forced to retreat until being resupplied. Ingenuity had to fill these gaps: on one occasion a witness saw a khaki line of Paulista soldiers crouched behind a trench under its black and white flag, firing their rifles and waving *matracas* (locally made rattles) to simulate the sound of machine gun fire in an attempt to repel an attack.[27]

Once the revolt spread, the economy of São Paulo was set on a war-footing, and practically all of the local society became involved. Women volunteered to work for the Red Cross and in factories: thousands of them served meals for the troops in the Soldier's House or participated in the 'Gold for São Paulo' campaign, collecting large quantities of jewellery and gold teeth donated by around 80,000 people.[28]

more than about 35,000 troops at the same time – and even this figure included non-armed, support troops.[26]

Even more critical was the lack of ammunition. The Paulistas' deposits had about six million bullets at the start of the war, and the factories of São Paulo are known to have manufactured at least as many throughout the conflict. This figure might appear exorbitant but

Casa do Soldado (House of the Soldier) in Barão de Itapetininga Street with visiting Paulista soldiers. (Coleção Paulo Florençano, Taubaté, via Donato)

Paulista propaganda poster asking for recruits: 'You have a duty to honour. Ask your conscience.' (Coleção Paulo Florençano, Taubaté, via Donato)

A Paulista postcard for the Military Mail. (Arquivo Nosso Século, via Donato)

Weapons and Equipment

As they drew upon the same arsenals, both sides used the same weapons. The main rifles were various models of Mauser, such as the old M1895 or the 7mm calibre M1908, but there was also the rare – yet modern – M1922. These Mausers, with a range of 1,000 metres, could be fitted with a bayonet. Smaller quantities of Czechoslovak-made VZ24s were available too, and a few volunteers and reservists went into battle armed with Lee Enfields cut down as carbines. The officers were usually armed with semi-automatic pistols like the M1906 DWM Luger and Mauser C96 (or its Astra copy made in Spain); a few had Colt revolvers from the time of the American Civil War. Hand grenades were mostly of the Mills type: this was a version that could be thrown by hand out to about 20–24 metres, or when fired from a rifle they could reach 80–100 metres.[29]

Automatic weapons were scarce. The most common were Hotchkiss heavy machine guns, with a rate of fire of 250–400 rounds per minute over a range of 2,000–4,000 metres. Light machine guns were foremost of the Hotchkiss M1922 type of 6.5mm or 8mm calibre: they had a rate of fire of between 60 and 200 rounds per minute. A few Madsen 7mm machine guns (with a rate of fire of 300 rounds per minute), some Colt and Maxim heavy machine guns and sub-machine guns, a few ZBs and various others are mentioned by different sources, but none was available in significant quantities.[30]

Heavy weapons of the Brazilian Army mainly consisted of guns made by well-known German and French companies such as Krupp and Schneider. At first, Krupp managed to close the access to his competitor and got the first order for rapid-firing 75mm L/28 cannons. Sources differ widely over the exact number delivered, some citing only 36 pack artillery and 108 field pieces and others 232 of the L/28 type pieces. In 1907, Brazil also acquired 24 Krupp-made L/14 mountain

A Paulista armoured flamethrower car being tested in Lorena, under Captain Saldanha. (Waldemar Martins Ferreira Filho, via Donato)

An armoured tractor improvised by the Paulistas. Notable are steel wheels, but also the machine gun positions and the absence of tracks. (Biblioteca Municipal Mário de Andrade, Careta 24.09.1932, via Donato)

guns, that the Paulistas deployed mounted on trains for support of their units.[32]

Overall, as of July 1932, the Paulistas operated at last 12 75mm Krupp guns, four 105mm and 22 75mm Schneider guns and a handful of other types. These 42 guns confirmed as operated by the rebels faced at least 150, perhaps 250, guns operated by the Federal Army: 100 of these were concentrated in the Detachment of the East alone.[33]

With regards to armour, the sole Tank Company of the Brazilian Army, equipped with Renault FT-17s from the Great War, was dissolved in March 1932. However, enough of these remained intact and operational to form a section of three 'assault tanks' that appeared on the Mantiqueira Tunnel Front: one was armed with a 37mm cannon and two with machine guns.[34] For their part, the Paulistas constructed several armoured trains – designated from 1 to 6, the last of which was deployed in Paraíba – each equipped with one 75mm cannon, 12 rifles and four machine guns installed in revolving turrets. Moreover, the Paulistas are known to have built several improvised armoured trucks and tractors, all equipped with machine guns, and one equipped with a flamethrower. However, except for the trains, none of these seem to have been deployed in combat.[35] Finally, the Paulistas also devised a mortar called the *sapinhos*, capable of firing 2kg bombs over a range of 800 metres.[36]

In terms of uniforms, both sides were very similar: the standard light khaki of

guns, and a year later another 30 howitzers of 105mm calibre. These were used to replace ancient Grusonwerke M1892 53mm cannons, Maxim Nordenfeldt M1889s and Canet M1890 howitzers of 75mm and 100mm calibre left over from the 19th century. The First World War prevented Brazil from the acquisition of another batch of Krupp-made guns ordered in 1913. Thus, the French company Schneider exploited the opportunity to sell 100 M1918 75mm howitzers, while St Chamod secured an order for 12 M1920 75mm howitzers a year later.[31] Both the Federal Army and the Paulistas operated Stokes Mortars and some coastal artillery, such as Schneider Canet 150mm

the Brazilian Army with brown or black leather boots, and olive grey-green belts and ammunition pockets. To help identify their combatants, the Paulistas began using white scarves worn around the neck. Furthermore, and despite the fact that the Federals wore canvas helmets, with only high-ranking officers wearing steel helmets, most of the Paulista soldiers were equipped with locally made copies of the British Mk I helmet, copies of the French M1915 Adrian helmet or a local variant of the Adrian with a dome at the top instead of the typical crest.[37] There is still a widespread belief that the Paulistas wore cork helmets, but photographs provide clear evidence in this matter, as do the testimonies of the veterans. Furthermore, Irany Paraná do Brasil

A Paulista *sapinho* locally made mortar. (Instituto Histórico e Geográfico de São Paulo, via Donato)

Drawing of a Paulista soldier with an Adrian 1915-type helmet with a dome instead of a crest. (Arquivo Nosso Século, via Donato)

still refers to this battalion's 'steel helmets', described as 'not being anatomical', little, light and loose: probably, these were a local version of the Mk I – subsequently replaced by one of better shape and weight, probably based on the Adrian design.[38]

3

BRAZILIAN AVIATION

Although it is generally accepted that the first aircraft to make a controlled flight was invented by the Wright brothers in the USA, this should probably be attributed to a Brazilian, Alberto Santos Dumont. This engineer had built several heavier-than-air machines capable of flying without external means. In 1905, he designed the prototype 14-Bis, equipped with an engine, which was built and tested on 12 September 1906 and rose up to an altitude of 7 metres and 60 centimetres. Admittedly, this was a somewhat limited achievement,

A Paulista soldier writing home. Note the Adrian 1915 helmet. (Coleão Paulo Florençano, Taubaté, via Donato)

but on 23 October the same aeroplane was retested in front of a crowd at the Campo de Bagatelle in Paris: this event was filmed by pioneer Pathé, who was thus able to document a flight of 60 metres at an altitude of up to 3 metres. After thus earning himself the award sponsored by Archdeacon, Dumont went on to make a flight of 220 metres, winning the prize from the Aero Club of France in November of the same year. However, in 1908 the Wright brothers claimed the paternity of the invention for themselves, claiming that their Flyer 1 travelled over 36.5 metres in 1903 – a fascinating experience that, however, was conducted in secret, never filmed nor reported to the international press, and only documented with one photograph. Moreover, the Wright machine required a favourable wind and a catapult to fly, and its first publicly tested prototype appeared only in 1907. Thus, even if the Wright brothers were the first to get airborne in a construction of that kind, their aeroplane required an external means of aid to fly and should thus be sorted into the category of aircraft precursors – like the ill-fated Pilcher from England of 1899.

Considering all of this, Santos Dumont's suicide during the Paulista War, provoked by him seeing that his creation was used to kill other Brazilians, was particularly tragic.[1]

The Birth, Death and Rebirth of the Brazilian Air Service

The dispute over who was the first to construct and fly an aeroplane aside, the Aero Club of Brazil was established by 1911 and the Brazilian School of aviation in 1914. It was during the latter year that the Brazilian armed forces made the first use of aeroplanes for combat purposes, during the Contestado War. The Naval Aviation was established and its first military flying school came into being in 1916. Three years later – and with the help of the French Military Mission – the Military School of Aviation was established at Campo dos Afonsos, in Rio de Janeiro, then the capital of the country. Nevertheless, an air force as an independent branch within the Army was established only on 13 January 1927. Its first director served as the Chief-of-Staff to future General Pedro Aurélio de Góis Monteiro, who in 1932 would be in

Santos Dumont flying in his 14-Bis prototype in the Campo de Bagatelle, Paris, in 1906. (Daróz)

A Potez 25 TOE with pilot Captain João Negrão, a firefighter from the São Paulo Public Force turned aviator. (Daróz)

of snot, shaking and vomiting in a corner, entirely unable to overcome the appearance of the aircraft above them'.[2]

Paradoxically, the creation of the Brazilian Air Force advanced in the São Paulo area much faster than anywhere else in Brazil: there, it came into being by 1913. However, this organisation was dissolved on Vargas's order in 1930, amid rising concerns that it might turn against the central government. Thus, once the Paulista War erupted, the rebels had to start from scratch and improvise their air force for the war of 1932.[3]

What could be described as the 'Brazilian Air Force elsewhere' had only about 30 aircraft, and there is a never-ending dispute between professional researchers and enthusiasts over exactly how many were intact and how many operational as of July 1932, the exact quantities per type and their organisation. By deducing from all of the available sources, it is possible to provide a review as listed in Table 2.

Combat Squadron: The Potez 25 TOE

The premier unit of the Brazilian Air Force in 1932 was the Combat Squadron, which operated the main fighter-bomber type deployed by both parties: the two-seat Potez 25 TOE. Capable of reaching a maximum speed of 215km/h, this was armed with four machine guns: two Vickers 7.7mm synchronised with the propeller and two Dame 7.7mm on a rotating turret operated by the observer-gunner. In addition to its machine guns, the Potez 25 TOE could carry up to 240kg of bombs. As well as its powerful armament, it proved itself to be reliable and was not only used for ground attacks, but also as a heavy fighter. The only aerial victory achieved during the Paulista War came as a result of a clash between two aircraft of this type.

The Potez 25 TOE was superseded by the faster and more manoeuvrable NiD.72 and Falcons operated by the Paulistas: subsequently, it was relegated to operations of secondary importance and gradually replaced by the Wacos. While diverse sources usually report on the availability of 10–12 airframes, careful cross-examination of available evidence has shown that only eight saw any action – including two operated by the Paulistas: this figure matches the official one of six, as provided in the Memoranda of 12 and 13

command of the main front of the war, and also advocated for the use of aviation in the campaign: the man knew what he was talking about.

Indeed, the role of military aviation was vital for the conduct of the Paulista War. The effectiveness of contemporary combat aircraft was admittedly extremely limited, and their attacks produced – at most – about a half a dozen dead and wounded. They did kill a lot of fish in the local rivers, resulting in the mockery that the Brazilian Air Force would have served best 'for hunting and fishing' purposes. However, the psychological effects of even these early, feeble air raids were devastating. Whenever the 'tomato-red' Waco aeroplanes (nicknamed *vermelinhos*) appeared, panic seized the rebel troops, prompting them to leave their trenches without a fight: this included not only the novices, as might be expected, but even the tough and courageous, highly decorated veterans regularly turned into a 'weeping bunch

Table 2: Brazilian Federal Army Aviation, 1932 (Units marked in bold joined the mutiny.)

State	Unit	Strength	Active (plate #)	Repairing (plate #)	Type	Role	Notes
Rio do Janeiro	Combat Squadron	9	A-114		Po-25 TOE	Fighter-Bomber	
			A-115		Po-25 TOE	Fighter-Bomber	
			A-117		Po-25 TOE	Fighter-Bomber	
			A-211		Po-25 TOE	Fighter-Bomber	
			A-216		Po-25 TOE	Fighter-Bomber	
			A-217		Po-25 TOE	Fighter-Bomber	
				A-111	Po-25 TOE	Fighter-Bomber	Useless
				A-119	Po-25 TOE	Fighter-Bomber	Useless
				A-214	Po-25 TOE	Fighter-Bomber	Useless
São Paulo		**2**	**A-116**		**Po-25 TOE**	**Fighter-Bomber**	
			A-212		**Po-25 TOE**	**Fighter-Bomber**	
Rio do Janeiro	Training Squadron	3			Curtiss Fledging	Training	Unarmed
					Curtiss Fledging	Training	Unarmed
					Curtiss Fledging	Training	Unarmed
		4	M		Waco 240A	Fighter-Bomber	'Military Waco', armed
			C-1		Waco CSO/ 225	Fighter-Bomber	Mail aircraft, later armed
			C-3		Waco CSO/225	Fighter-Bomber	Mail aircraft, later armed. Deserted to the Paulistas, known as Waco Green
			C-4		Waco CSO/225	Fighter-Bomber	Mail aircraft, later armed
São Paulo		**2**	**C-2**		**Waco CSO/225**	**Fighter-Bomber**	**Mail aircraft, later armed**
			C-5		**Waco CSO/225**	**Fighter-Bomber**	**Mail aircraft, later armed**
Rio do Janeiro	Military School	2	K-422		NiD.72	Fighter	
			K-423		NiD.72	Fighter	Deserted to the Paulistas
		2		K-621	Amiot 122 BP3	Bomber	Not cited in the sources. Being repaired
			K-624		Amiot 122 BP3	Bomber	
		3	K-611		LeO 253 Bn.4	Heavy Bomber	Not used. No trained crew available
			K-612		LeO 253 Bn.4	Heavy Bomber	Not used. No trained crew available
			K-613		LeO 253 Bn.4	Heavy Bomber	Not used. No trained crew available
		6	3003		DH-60T Moth	Recce, liaison	Unarmed
			3010		DH-60T Moth	Recce, liaison	Unarmed
			K-141		DH-60T Moth	Recce, liaison	Unarmed
			K-143		DH-60T Moth	Recce, liaison	Unarmed
			K-150		DH-60T Moth	Recce, liaison	Unarmed
			K-152		DH-60T Moth	Recce, liaison	Unarmed
		3			PO-33	Training	Unarmed
		5			MS 130 Et.2	Training	Unarmed
		5			MS.147E.p .-2	Training	Unarmed
		1			Caudron C.59	Training	Unarmed
		1	K-231		Caudron C.140	Training	Unarmed
		2			Schreck FBA 17Ht2	Training	Unarmed

July by the Aviation Director, Aranha da Silva.[4] According to the same source, they were grouped into two 'squadrons' of three aircraft each: it is possible that this was actually still the same Combat Squadron but subdivided into two flights.[5]

Since 1930, the Brazilian Air Force had operated a detachment based at São Paulo. Two years later, this had only two Potezs, both of which were taken over by the Paulistas and were to form the backbone of their combat aviation early on, before Curtiss Falcons were acquired from Chile.[6]

Training Squadron and Mail-Planes: The Wacos

As of 1932, the Training Squadron of the Brazilian Air Force consisted of perhaps three Curtiss Fledging unarmed aircraft and six Wacos: only one of the latter was armed, while the other five were originally destined to serve as mail-planes. From the Wacos available at the start of the war, C-1, C-3 and C-4 (all unarmed Waco 225/CSOs), and M (an armed Waco 240A) remained with the Federals in Rio: C-2 and C-5 (both unarmed 225/CSOs) were taken up by the rebels.[7]

The Waco 225s (or CSOs) were tandem-type sport-biplanes: while unarmed, they offered enough space for the installation of a twin Colt/Browning 0.30 machine gun at the expanse of the front (passenger) seat. Brazil acquired several kits enabling exactly such a modification, even if their number was not enough to adapt every available airframe. Moreover, because these kits were located in Rio, only the aircraft retained by the Air Force could be modified that way: this was not possible for the two Wacos based in São Paulo and taken over by the Paulistas.[8] Still, the armed Waco C-3 was then flown to the rebel side by a defector – promptly improving the combat capability of the São Paulo-based rebel aviation by a third: the aircraft in question was probably painted in green subsequently and nicknamed *Waco Verde* (Green Waco). The other two examples flown by the Paulistas could barely defend themselves against their Federal-flown counterparts, but they all were equipped to carry a US Army-made A3 bomb-carrier under the fuselage, capable of carrying up to 140kg.[9]

At 210km/h, the Wacos had a similar maximum speed to the Potez. However, thanks to their lighter design, they weighed only 920kg, compared to 2,558kg of their primary rival. Thus, even if powered by an engine providing only 168–179Kw, as opposed to the 357Kw of the 25 TOE, they had a better power-to-weight ratio and were more manoeuvrable. Moreover, Wacos were cheaper: correspondingly, the Federals purchased 15 additional examples during the war (and many more afterwards), and they flew a host of ground attack sorties. Still, due to deficiencies in several of the available aircraft, not all the Wacos were better than the Potez. This was especially valid for the examples operated by the Paulistas. Out of about 10–12 Waco 225/CSOs that eventually entered service modified to carry machine guns the majority only served as bombers, as their MG.40 7mm machine guns used projectiles larger than the size of the cartridge case, causing them to frequently jam after only firing a few shots.[10]

Another issue troubling all the Wacos was their limited range of about 868km. Although longer than that of the Potez 25 TOE (600km), it was still inadequate and forced both sides to frequently operate them from forward operating locations, such as Resende, Lorena or Pouso Alegre, amongst others.

The Military School: NiD.72 Fighters and Amiot Bombers

Paradoxically, the Military Aviation School was not limited to having outdated or secondary aircraft but included brand-new equipment, as this was required to familiarise future pilots with it. As a result, this unit was actually well-armed and would soon join combat.

The standard US Army A-3 bomb kit installed below the fuselage of a Waco 225/CSO/240. (Waco, via Ray Brandly)

The very basic control panel of the Waco, that included merely the speed, a compass, oil temperature, oil pressure and propeller revolutions. (Daróz)

A two-seat Waco 225/CTO armed with a two-0.30 machine-gun kit occupying the co-pilot's seat. (Waco, via Ray Brandly)

The best fighters of the Paulista War were two Nieuport Delage NiD.72s. With a maximum speed of 260km/h and a 447Kw engine (while weighing only 1,471kg), they had an excellent power-to-weight ratio and easily outclassed both the Potez and the Waco. Indeed, the NiD.72s could reach an operational ceiling of 8,200 metres (compared to the 5,500 metres of the Potez) and thus surprise their opponents by diving upon them from above, in turn gaining higher speed and then easily avoiding a counter-attack – the so-called 'bounce' manoeuvre. Each of the NiDs was armed with a twin Vickers 7.7mm, synchronised with their propellers. Their main drawback was their critically short ange: at 400km, this was far too little to enable them any extended patrolling activity, and it forced the Brazilians to almost exclusively fly them from forward operating bases. While initially both NiD.72s (serials K-422 and K-423) were operated by the Federals, one of their pilots eventually defected to the Paulistas.[11]

Another model from the Military School was the Amiot 122 BP3, about which different sources disagree on whether there were one or two samples. Considering that this author has identified only the K-621 in action, it is likely that the other – serial K-624 – was either non-operational or undergoing repairs. The Amiot 122 BP3 was a three-seater bomber with a speed equal to the Potezs and Wacos, about 205km/h, heavily armed with five Vickers and Lewis .303/7.7mm machine guns (two synchronised with the propeller, two mobile in the rear and one ventral), and capable of carrying a load of 800kg of bombs under the wings and fuselage. As such, it was the second-largest bomber of this war, after the Savoia-Marchetti SM.55. On top of that it had great range, about 1,000km, which allowed it to deploy from safer aerodromes, well away from the battlefield: unsurprisingly, the fleet never left its base in Dos Afonsos outside Rio. Of course, with its 4,500kg weight and 485Kw engine, the Amiot was less manoeuvrable than the Potez and easy prey for the faster NiD.72 and Falcons, and – sometimes – even for Wacos.[12]

There are different opinions on the number of available airframes for the Lioré-et-Olivier LeO 253 Bn.4 heavy night bomber, ranging from one to three (registered as K-611 to K-613). This was a powerful aircraft powered by a twin engine with an output of 485Kw, reaching maximum speeds of 230km/h and a ceiling of 8,000 meters. As such, it could easily avoid Paulista Wacos and Potezs, but not the NiD and Falcons. Its great range, 1,500km, made it ideal for strategic bombing deep inside enemy territory. However, the LeO 253 was only armed with three 7.5mm machine guns, and despite weighing 9,560kg, could only carry 700kg of bombs – i.e. less than the Amiot. Even then, the lack of crews qualified to operate it rendered this – potentially precious – aircraft surplus: it was kept in reserve and never flown during the Paulista War.[13]

Army and Navy Moths and Avros

Another type widely used by the Military School of the Army was the famous de Havilland DH.60T Moth. While diverse sources usually cite the availability of up to 11 such aircraft, the existence of just six was confirmed through their registrations (3003, 3010, K141, K143, K150 and K152) these were probably the only examples available for operations. The Moth was not for combat, but a training aircraft, and thus poorly powered and slow: the engine produced only 75Kw, the maximum speed was a mere 135km/h and the range limited to 490km. As such, it was easy prey for the Potezs and Wacos. Unsurprisingly, their pilots rarely ventured away from their bases, and only flew short missions.[14]

Other types were operated by the Military School for training purposes during the war, but never performed any combat missions. These included three old Potez 33s, five Morane Saulnier MS.130 Et2s, five Morane Saulnier MS.147E.p-2s, one Cauldron C.59, one Cauldron C.140 (registration K231) and two Schreck FBA.17Ht2s.[15]

In addition to the Moths operated by the Army, there were another six operated by the Naval Aviation (registrations 1-1-1, 1-1-2, 1-1-6, 1-1-7, 1-1-9 and 1.1.19), out of a theoretical total of about nine to 12 aircraft. Later on, the Federals would arrange these to operate in groups of three aircraft, two of these to be armed (one with a machine gun and one with bombs), while one was equipped with a radio.[16]

The other type operated by the Naval Aviation were six obsolete Avro 504 N/Os (registrations 441 to 446).[17] However, it remains unknown how many of these were operational by the time the war began. Slightly more potent than Moths, they could reach a speed of 161km/h, but had a short range (only 420km) and low operational ceiling (4,875m), were mostly made of wood and were only armed with a single Vickers 7.7mm machine gun. As far as is known, they were allocated to the front line of Mato Grosso until the arrival of the Paulista Falcons forced the Federals to keep them away from the battlefield.[18]

SM.55 and Martin PM 1-B Naval Bombers

Another unit of the Naval Aviation – the Patrol Aircraft Mixed Flotille – operated two or three Martin PM 1-B amphibious aircraft (registrations 111 and 112), and six or seven Savoia-Marchetti S.55As (those designated as 1, 4, 6, 8, 10 and 11 were mentioned in various reports during the war). Out of these, only three (6, 10 and 11) were repaired and operational at the start of the war. Overall, Brazilian Naval Aviation thus had only two PMs and three SM.55s ready for action as of July 1932.

With regards to the SM.55s, there is little doubt that – despite their awkward design – they were the most advanced bombers in all of Latin America at the time. Emerging in 1924, they won several records for speed, load, altitude and distance, and were deployed to cross the South Atlantic for the first time by João Ribeiro Barros in the aircraft nicknamed *Jahú* (preserved in Brazil to this day). The SM.55 was powered by two engines of 418Kw, one of which pulled and the other pushed, for a maximum speed of 280km/h. As such, it was next-to-impossible to catch for both the NiDs and the Paulista Falcons. The only weakness of the SM.55s was their low operational ceiling, at 5,000m: this did make it possible for interceptors to attack them in a dive, gaining extra speed as they went, but this was a complicated and dangerous manoeuvre even for the Falcons. Moreover, the Italian amphibian was heavily armed with a total of four Lewis machine guns installed in two barbettes on the front and the rear, and thus de-facto invulnerable to interception. The SM.55 could carry up to 2,000kg of bombs (twice the load of the LeO and Amiot), and its range was outstanding: it could reach over 4,500km and thus raid even targets deep within enemy territory.[19]

Three Morane Saulnier MS.147 E.p.-2 trainers parked in line, with numbers K-130, K-129 and K-217 visible. They did not see action in the war. (Daróz)

Table 3: Brazilian Naval Aviation in 1932

State	Unit	Number of Units	Active (plate #)	Repairing (plate #)	Type	Role	Notes
Rio do Janeiro	Mixed Patrol Aircraft Flotille	2	111		Martin PM-1	Recce, bomber	Seaplane
			112		Martin PM-1	Recce, bomber	Seaplane
		6	1		SM.55	Heavy bomber	Seaplane
			4		SM.55	Heavy bomber	Seaplane
			8		SM.55	Heavy bomber	Seaplane
				6	SM.55	Heavy bomber	Seaplane
				10	SM.55	Heavy bomber	Seaplane
				11	SM.55	Heavy bomber	Seaplane
Rio do Janeiro	1st Observation Division	4	1-0-2		O2U-2 Corsair	Fighter	
			1-0-3		O2U-2 Corsair	Fighter	
			1-0-4		O2U-2 Corsair	Fighter	
			1-0-6		O2U-2 Corsair	Fighter	
Rio do Janeiro	Others	6	1.1.1		DH-60 Moth	Recce	Later armed forming 3 aircraft groups (radio, bombs & gun)
			1.1.2		DH-60 Moth	Recce	Later armed forming 3 aircraft groups
			1.1.6		DH-60 Moth	Recce	Later armed forming 3 aircraft groups
			1.1.7		DH-60 Moth	Recce	Later armed forming 3 aircraft groups
			1.1.9		DH-60 Moth	Recce	Later armed forming 3 aircraft groups
			1.1.19		DH-60 Moth	Recce	Later armed forming 3 aircraft groups
		2			Avro-504	Recce	Moved to Mato Grosso

The Martin PM stood no comparison to the SM.55: despite having two 391Kw engines, it had a maximum a speed of just 184km/h, a service ceiling of only 3,300m and was armed with only two Lewis 0.303 machine guns. As such, it was easy prey for all interceptors deployed in this war. On the positive side, it could carry four 104kg bombs under its wings over a range of 2,100km. Unsurprisingly, for most of the Paulista War they operated along the coast.[20]

Navy Corsair Fighters And Paulista Falcons

The second-best fighters of the Paulista War were four O2U-2A Corsairs (registrations 102, 103, 104 and 106) of the 1st Observation Division of the Brazilian Navy.[21] Powered by a 447Kw engine while weighing 2,161kg, they had a power-to-weight ratio equivalent to that of the Waco and proved marginally more manoeuvrable, even if not able to compete with the Paulista-operated NiDs. Therefore, their pilots tended to disengage if sighting the latter, climb and bounce from above, exploiting their slight advantage in maximum speed (269km/h). Ultimately, all the Potezs, Wacos and Falcons operated by the Paulistas proved unable to combat them.

Each of the four Corsairs was armed with two 7.62mm machine guns (one fore and the other aft, operated by the gunner) and could carry up to 226.5kg of bombs over a range of 1,094km. As such they proved capable of providing top

The excellent Savoia-Marchetti SM.55A: a fast and well-armed twin-float flying boat, and the best bomber of the war. (SDM via Sergio Luis dos Santos)

A Martin PM 1-B Seaplane, armed with bombs under the lower wing and nose, with no sign of machine guns installed. Note also the personal badge and the plate number 1-P-2, a pre-war or post-war code. (SDM via Sergio Luis dos Santos)

All of the available Naval seaplanes in line, the six SM.55s on the left and the three Martin PMs on the right side, probably at Galeão after the war. (SDM via Sergio Luis dos Santos)

A line of Corsair V-65Bs acquired after the war, a variant very similar to the four Corsair O2-Us operated by the Navy during the conflict. These were, with the NiD.72, the best fighter aircraft of the war. (Vought)

'*Taguató*' and '*José Mário*'. The latter arrived at Mato Grosso just in time to make a single mission, while the '*Taguató*' was eventually severely damaged in São Paulo when trying to coordinate the machine guns with the propeller blade.

The Falcon had a 324Kw engine, while weighing 1,972kg, and thus had a slightly lesser power-to-weight ratio than its rivals. It could reach a maximum speed of 224km/h, which was better than that of the Wacos and Potezs, but insufficient to catch the SM.55s, Corsairs or NiD.72s. At 4,600m, its maximum operational ceiling also made the Falcon susceptible to bouncing. However, it proved an excellent fighter-bomber and, had the Paulistas managed to get more than four of them operational, they could have swept the skies clear of the Federal Air Force.[23]

Colours and Markings

Contrary to what is often reported, as of 1932, the aircraft of the Brazilian Air Force wore roundels in the national colours of green, yellow and blue on their wings. The nowadays well-known Brazilian star was officially approved only in 1940. Similarly, the two-colour fuselage and/or rudder bands reported by some sources were officially approved by the Bulletin for Military Aviation only on 28 February 1934. Before that date – and thus during the Paulista War – the aircraft were instead marked by three vertical bands, with blue at the leading edge of the rudder or its interior part, then the yellow and finally green on the trailing

cover even for bombers striking targets deep over enemy territory – as during raids by Amiots against Paulista positions in the Paraíba Valley, or for SM.55 attacks on Santos.[22]

To counter the Corsairs, towards the end of the war the Paulistas acquired 10 Curtiss Falcon O1-Es from Chile. One was written off during the delivery flight, while another was 'spent' as a 'commission' to Paraguay in exchange for their transit permission. Eventually, only four actually saw any service, nicknamed '*Kavuré-Y*', '*Kyri-Kyri*', edge of the rudder. Curiously, photographs show that these colours were often applied in the opposite order, with blue on the exterior of the rudder. Moreover, in some cases green and blue bands were painted next to each other, with no yellow between them; some aircraft – such as the Avros – seem to have received roundels with the yellow colour in the centre.[24]

A Curtiss D-12 Falcon, acquired via Chile by the Paulista Aviation. If all 10 of them had been available at the same time, perhaps the result of the war could have been entirely different. (Daróz)

That said, the principal colour applied on aircraft was olive green for all the machines operated by the Army, and white or silver for all those operated by the Navy. The Savoias were an exception; they were sometimes described as painted in beige or light orange, or – like the Jahú flown over the Atlantic – painted in red overall. The Wacos were usually painted in red overall, and thus became known as the *vermelinhos* (little reds). For the Corsairs, there are reports that their top wing was painted in yellow with a blue band on the fuselage, but this remains unconfirmed by photographs, other than a few taken only after the end of the Paulista War.

The Paulistas usually retained the original colours of their aircraft – especially so for the Wacos. An exception was the armed Waco C-3, which was completely painted in green, though probably not in olive green. The red-painted Wacos received some white and black bands, and flags below their wings, to distinguish them from the Federals, which carried roundels in that place. The Potezs were left in olive green, but had their original markings overpainted: they received a vertical white band down their fuselage. Their roundels were overpainted, and the rudders painted entirely in green. The Falcons arrived in Brazil painted white or silver overall, with their designation on the engine cowling, and a black-white-black vertical band on the fuselage. The sole Paulista-operated NiD-72 was painted in the same fashion, though ironically it became known as the '*Negrinho*' ('Little Black'). Finally, there are numerous reports that early during the war the Paulista aircraft had received black roundels and a white band on the wings and the fuselage. Others reportedly received a red flag on their wings. It is possible that these were the civilian types which were never used for combat operations.[25]

4

THE PAULISTA UPRISING

General Bertholdo Klinger was an able commander at regiment level and was the most successful leader of the government troops in the Lieutenants Revolt of 1925. He failed to lead the troops of his Mato Grosso Brigade, arriving alone without any soldiers, and this failure forced the date of the Paulista rebellion to be moved forwards. Then, as the Constitutionalist supreme commander, he showed a fateful lack of initiative that doomed the rebel cause. (Daróz)

Led by old General Isidoro Dias Lopes, the Constitutionalist conspirators originally fixed the date of their coup attempt for 20 July. The idea was that this would enable their allies in the states of Rio de Janeiro, Minas Gerais and Rio Grande do Sul to also prepare. However, two events precipitated their plan. First, after being informed about the clashes and demonstrations that were taking place in São Paulo, the Federal government sent General Pereira de Vasconcelos to impose order in the city, and on 7 July he was already on his way. Given the risk that Vasconcelos would dismantle the revolt before it could spread, the conspirators decided to react as soon as possible. Nevertheless, their 'inaction' exasperated General Bertoldo Klinger, commander of Mato Grosso Military District, who was also committed to the revolt. To enforce the coup, on 8 July 1932, Klinger wrote a provocative letter to the Federal Minister of War, General Espirito Santo Cardoso, calling him incompetent. He was promptly dismissed from his position – and thus free to lead the military aspect of the revolt, even without the promised 5,000 troops of the Mixed Brigade stationed in 'his' former district.

Klinger had proved himself the most brilliant tactician during the fighting against the Prestes Column in the revolutions of 1925–27. However, he was not as competent at the strategic level: his conduct of the Paulista War was to prove a fiasco at a very early stage. Before long, he was paralysed, taking next to no decisions and leaving the local commanders to act on their own and without appropriate coordination.

Meanwhile, on 8 July, the conspirators who had to organise the uprisings in the north of Brazil met at the Hotel Gloria to convince the Governor of Rio Grande do Sul, Flores da Cunha, to join the revolt.

General Isidoro Dias Lopes, a 'conservative' and head of the Paulista conspirators that led the São Paulo uprising. (Daróz)

They decided to advance the date of the revolt to 14 July. However, the arrival of the news of the dismissal of Klinger changed all of the plans again, and the Constitutionalists met once more on 9 July in a private building, which had been empty for some time and served as the headquarters of the revolution, located on Sergipe 37 Street in São Paulo. Presiding over the meeting was Isidoro Dias Lopes, who proposed initiating the revolt that same day, despite the risk of short-circuiting the preparations, before their allies from the north and the south could meet them. Feeling forced by the circumstances, the conspirators finally agreed to launch the uprising late on 9 July. The signal would be 'Sergipe', and the answer '37'.

Colonel Euclides Figueiredo, commander of the Paulista FP, immediately assumed supreme command of the city of São Paulo and put his forces on alert. Civilians of the MMDC militia under Captain Antonio Pietscher occupied the telegraph and radio stations and reported to the municipal leaders of this organisation that they should trigger the revolt in their respective areas. Dario Machado's group would mobilise 80 trucks and cars to help accelerate and expand the uprising. Students affiliated to Perdizes Street, according to some, were the first to move, reaching the Law University. There, together with other students they established the 1st BMCP under Romão Gomes, commander of the FPP and the most successful commander among the Paulistas during the war. This unit was the genesis of the Constitutionalist Army. Moreover, the medical corps of the rebel army was organised at the Medicine University.[1] Although still not sure whether the coup was to become successful or not, the Paulista rebels were already preparing for war.

Aeroplanes and Troops for São Paulo (9/10 July)

At 21:00hrs local time, Figueiredo, commander of the rebels in the area, controlled the entire city, including all of the FPP under Colonel Marcondes Salgado. Next, Figueiredo went with Colonel Palimércio Resende to occupy the Military Region headquarters, located in Chácara de Carvalho. Once there, the guard let them enter, at 23:40hrs, so that – in agreement with Dias Lopes – Colonel Figueiredo assumed command of the 2nd Military Region and the 2nd Infantry Division. Simultaneously, the FPP Cavalry Regiment went to the Campo de Marte, where they discovered the unarmed Waco aircraft C-2 and C-5 inside a hangar of the Military Air Mail. On 11 July, the Paulistas attempted to install machine guns into the front cockpits of these tandem aircraft, but because of the improvised nature of the resulting installation there was a problem with synchronisation with the propellers. Eventually, as no other solution could be found, it was decided to leave the aircraft as they were, but to man them with a two-person crew and arm the 'passenger' with a machine gun.[2]

Shortly after, in the early hours of 10 July, 4th BC and 2nd BCP departed to bring 4th RI, located in Quitaúna, west of São Paulo, under their control. They encountered no resistance: on the contrary, this unit also joined the rebellion.[3] To quite some surprise, the Paulistas then found two Potezs, A-116 and A-212, parked on the nearby airfield.[4] Together with the two Wacos, these aircraft were to form the nucleus of the Constitucionalista Aviation. Furthermore, using both requisitions and voluntary deliveries, the rebels became capable of incorporating a number of civilian aircraft of the Club Bandeirantes and the São Paulo Aero-Club.[5] Specifically, from the Bandeirantes they obtained between one and three DH.60 Moths (owned by João de Costa and Raphael Chrysostomo de Oliveira), a Fleet (sold to the Club by Leigh Wade), a Curtiss JN-2 (donated by Captain Reynaldo Gonçalves, previously owned by Armando Bordallo), a Nieuport Ni-80,

Rebel students armed with Winchester rifles, seen after taking control of the Telefónica Company building. (Coleção Paulo Florençano, Taubaté, via Donato)

18–22 aircraft, only four were useful for combat purposes, the two Potezs and two Wacos, and of those the two Wacos, had major problems with installing their machine guns.[7]

Still, the situation for the rebels was hopeful. On the same day, 10 July, at 15:00hrs, the Governor of São Paulo State, Pedro de Toledo, informed Getúlio Vargas about the triumph of the revolt, joined the rebels and then resigned.[8]

Campo de Marte, São Paulo City, in the 1930s, which was turned into the largest air base for the rebel aviation. Here the Paulistas found their two first combat aircraft, Wacos C-2 and C-5. (Daróz)

10–16 July 1932: An Offensive that is not an Offensive

While the Paulistas were quick in securing the city of São Paulo, the revolt was spreading outside the metropolis too. At 08:30hrs, the first troops went to board

Colonel Euclides Figueiredo, with his Paulista white handkerchief. He was the commander of the São Paulo State *Força Publica* and ably controlled São Paulo City and the headquarters of the 2nd Division in the state. He assumed the command of this rebel unit and the forces in the Paraíba Valley, but his initial march against Rio was cancelled by General Klinger. (Daróz)

The Governor of São Paulo, Pedro de Toledo who, despite being appointed by Vargas, joined the rebels. Drawing by Belmonte, in *Folha da Noite*. (Folha de São Paulo, via Donato)

a Morane Saulnier MS-29 and an unidentified Breda (owned by the widow of Vasco Cinquini). From the Aero-Club they collected one or two Henriot 410s, and from the *Club Aviação Jaboticabal* one or two Ni-81s and one Caudron 93-Bis (or G.III). Finally, the Campo de Marte provided another Caudron (owned by Fritz Roesller), a monoplane Monocoupé, an Avro C.III and a Savoia-Marchetti S.56, which curiously had been requisitioned from a pilot who fought with the Federals, Lieutenant Francisco 'Maluco' Melo.[6] However, of these

Potez A-212, known as *Nosso Potez* (*Our Potez*), having just been captured in Quitaúna by the rebels. In this picture taken in Campo de Marte at the beginning of the war you can see all the original aviators of the São Paulo Força Publica. This was the only aircraft that downed an enemy aircraft in combat during the war, the first such achievement in the Americas, but ended its days when destroyed in an accident. (Daróz)

a train to Rio de Janeiro, being hailed by the crowds. Led by Romào Gomes, they marched through the Largo de São Francisco. However, the order for the troops and successive trains was to not advance beyond the Sierra de Mantiqueira. The strategy behind this decision was to wait for the arrival of the Mineiros allies and the *Gaúchos* from Rio Grande do Sul, and not to make the revolt too prominent outside the area from which it originated.[9] Thus, the 1st BCP FPP, 2nd GIAP and 4th Squadron/2nd RCD slowly marched east, to Mogi das Cruces, with the intention to, later and if necessary, continue on to Rio. However, they did not move beyond that point. After forming the brigade-sized Major Agnelo Detachment, commanded by Agnelo de Sousa, and being reinforced by 2nd BCP and 4th BC, most of them were ordered

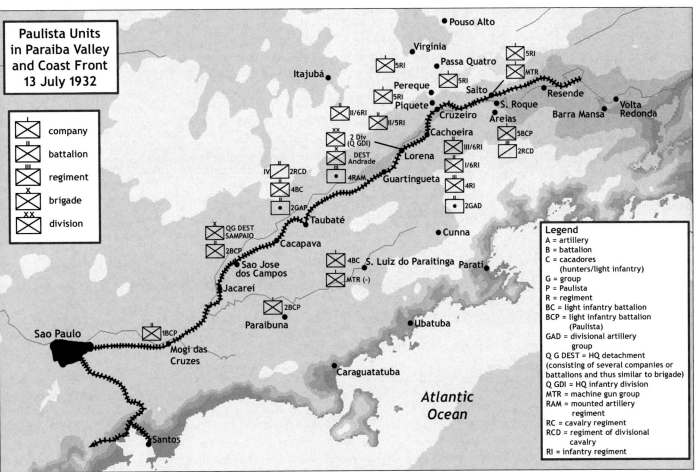

Based on Ramos, this map depicts the position of the Paulista units in the Paraíba Valley as of 13 July 1932. Detachments Sampaio (in São Jose de Campos) and Andrade (in Lorena) were in control of numerous minor formations. However, the Paulistas stopped at this point in time and did not attempt an advance on Rio de Janeiro. Notably, while marked as 'companies', all the machine-gun units were actually only sections and not of company strength. (Map by Tom Cooper)

decision was eased by the arrival of General Vasconcelos: he was sent by Góis Monteiro to recover control of the State of São Paulo, but, on arrival in Caçapava, at 16:00hrs, decided to join the rebels.

However, even once they sided with the rebellion, instead of being rushed in the direction of Rio de Janeiro, the troops of 5th RI were diverted north, to protect the entrance to Minas Gerais via the Mantiqueira Tunnel. Behind them, on 12 July, Colonel Euclides Figueiredo took command of the forces in the Paraíba Valley, which received the official designation 2nd Division in Operations (2nd DIO).

Through all of this time, the rearguard of the Agnelo-Sampaio Detachment remained

Paulista troops departing for the Paraíba front. Note, on the right, soldiers wearing British Mk I-type helmets and also some in canvas hats. (Coleção Paulo Florençanp, Taubaté, via Donato)

Governor Pedro de Toledo reviewing the Paulista troops before going to the front. (Arquivo Nosso Século, via Donato)

Colonel Euclides Figueiredo, commander of the Paulista 2nd Division in Operations (2nd DIO) that fought in the Paraíba Valley. (Waldemar Martins Ferreira Filho, via Donato)

to return to São Paulo. There, the command of the detachment was given to Colonel Antonio Paiva Sampaio. Meanwhile, their rearguard remained in Mogi, to monitor the railway from São Paulo to Rio. Eventually, an absurd situation developed: nobody issued – and thus nobody received – the order to move on the capital at the critical time.

Part of the hesitation by the conspirators was based on the necessity to find out what 5th RI would do – the unit garrisoning the entrance to the Paraíba Valey, which connects São Paulo with Rio. Eventually, this powerful unit joined the rebellion after some hesitation of the battalion commander in Lorena and the two in Caçapava. Their

in Mogi das Cruces, doing nothing. On 13 July, the detachment was concentrated again, and only a day later was 1st BCP ordered to start moving. On 14 July, after leaving behind a company of troops to garrison the place, the detachment moved east to Guaratinguetá. A day later, 2nd BCP continued to Cruzeiro, but stopped again to deploy its 3rd and 4th Companies to reinforce the 2nd Battalion of 5th RI in the Mantiqueira Tunnel.

On 16 July, a new unit – the Sampaio Detachment – was established from 2nd BCP. The unit then marched from São Jose dos Campos to

General Pereira de Vasconcelos, sent to Caçapava by Vargas to take control of 5th RI, but who crossed to the Paulista cause. (Waldemar Martins Ferreira Filho, via Donato)

The Federal 2nd BC, based in Sete Pontas, disembarking in Niteroi to protect the town. Note the cork helmet of the officer and the canvas caps for the troops. (Arquivo Nosso Século, via Donato)

Cruzeiro, where it took over control of two companies of 5th BCP, the 3rd Battalion of 5th RI and 2nd GIAP. Finally, instead of being sent east, the detachment was diverted to the Mantiqueira Tunnel, north of the valley.

In similar fashion, many other units that joined the rebellion spent their first few days doing nothing. For example, 6th RI remained in the barracks of 2nd Military Region, in São Paulo, supposedly to act as a reserve. Unsurprisingly, by the time the Paulistas finally realised their failure, and rushed the newly established Andrade Detachment in the direction of Rio, the Federal forces were already in position and ready.[10]

9–10 July 1932: Góis Monteiro Saving the Government in Rio

The above-mentioned series of – inexplicable – delays eventually enabled Getúlio Vargas and his aides to overcome the initial shock and prepare their forces for the defence. Indeed, in a surprising act of farsightedness, General Pedro Aurélio Góis Monteiro, commander of 1st Military Region, summoned his troops at the army base in Rio de Janeiro as early as 9 July, at 18:00hrs local time, before the uprising even began. All suspicious personnel were promptly detained and placed under observation. Thus, all the Paulistas within 1st RCD, 3rd RI, the Heavy Artillery Regiment (1st GIAP) and 2nd BC of 1st Infantry Division were out of action with a single blow.

Góis next ordered a company of 1st RI – reinforced with a section of heavy machine guns – to march on Barra de Pirai, link-up with the police of Rio de Janeiro and protect the tunnels on the railroad connecting the capital with São Paulo. Finally, he dispatched 1st RCD – commanded by Colonel Otávio Pires Coelho – to Caçapava, well inside São Paulo State.

Left: A view of General Tasso Fragoso inspecting the troops. We will never know if Fragoso was trying to protect Vargas in Rio or, on the contrary, was trying to make the offensive by the Paulistas easier. Finally, Góis Monteiro was able to cancel his orders. (Della Rosa, via Historia y Vida)

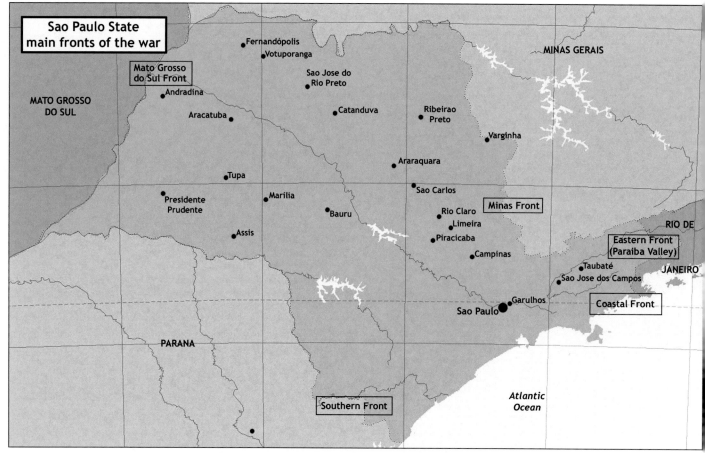

A map of São Paulo State with the main theatres of war. (Map by Tom Cooper)

Obviously, the Loyalists were not to show as much prudence as the rebels did.[11]

Of course, and as described above, General Vasconcelos' – supposedly similar – attempt to re-establish the control of 2nd Military Region in São Paulo was a scam: as soon as he arrived at the local HQ, he sided with the rebels. Nevertheless, the Federalist commanders were quick in reacting to it. As soon as Góis was informed about Vasconcelos' treachery, he ordered 1st RCD to occupy Resende. At this point in time, the Chief-of-Staff of the Brazilian Army, General Tasso Fragoso, intervened: he sympathised with the idea of 're-constitutionalisation' and thus attempted to cancel Góis' orders. On Fragoso's advice, Vargas himself ordered 1st RCD back to Rio. According to Pessoa, Góis' Chief-of-Staff, the argument that was used in Vargas's presence was that the city of São Paulo was already empty of troops, and that the rebellion was forcing the remaining loyalists out. While apparently a reasonable argument, thanks to Pessoa's intervention, Góis was not as easy to fool. After locating him in his house, at 04:00hrs, the general and his aide held an improvised meeting inside the bedroom of Góis' daughter while she was sleeping. They concluded that Tasso was behind the order for 1st RCD to withdraw and decided to ignore it. Thus, early the next morning not only this unit, but also 1st BC and 1st RI – both commanded by Colonel Cristovão Ferreira da Silva – marched into the Paraíba Valley.

Meanwhile, Góis Monteiro returned to the HQ in Rio, where he had a tough verbal exchange with Fragoso, in the presence of Vargas. Upon witnessing Góis' self-confidence, and facing his threat of resignation, he expressed his support. Góis Monteiro was promptly assigned the commander of the main front in the following war – later the 'Army Detachment of the East' – and put in control of both 1st and 4th Divisions, stationed in Rio and Minas Gerais. It was only years

later that Góis acknowledged that he was wrong in doubting Tasso Fragoso's good faith.[12]

Once free of Fragoso's interruptions and in command of the Army Detachment of the East, Góis continued his strategy of deploying as many troops as possible at greatest speed to the west and blocking the Paraíba Valley route. At 09:30hrs on 10 July, 1st RCD continued its march on Resende. Meanwhile, 3rd RI – commanded by Colonel Daltro Filho – followed it by train, with 1st BC – commanded by Colonel Colatino Maques – in its wake. Finally, 2nd RI – commanded by Colonel João Guedes Fontoura, who was actually a Paulista-sympathiser and had originally pledged to join the revolt – marched along the Rio–São Paulo highway, south of the valley, on the towns of Formosa and Bananal.[13]

The Government's Reaction in the Rest of Brazil

Even if his loyalty was suspected by Góis, who then found himself favoured by Vargas, General Tasso Fragoso retained his position of the Chief-of-Staff, and meanwhile played a crucial role in organising the Brazilian Army in other parts of the country. For example, to cover the approaches to Rio from the direction east of São Paulo, he arranged the deployment of the troops from 4th and 8th Military Regions. Nearly all of the units of 4th Military Region (mainly various elements of 4th Infantry Division) were ordered to march across the Sierra de Mantiqueira on Cruzeiro and Lorena in Paraíba, and thus block any possible Paulista advance on the capital. Afterwards, they were to move from Uberaba, home base of 6th BC, which was the only major element of 2nd Infantry Division not to join the mutiny, on Caçapava and Ribeirão Preto.[14]

Furthermore, Tasso Fragoso organised 6th Military Region (which controlled 24th, 25th, 26th and 27th BCs) and 7th Military Region (19th, 20th, 21st, 22nd, 23rd and 28th BCs) to redeploy some of

eir assets for the defence of Rio, and others into sectors around the
bellious state.[15]

Although all the related orders were followed as smoothly as
ossible, 4th Division nearly experienced a major disaster in the
açapava and Ribeirão Preto area. Basically, Tasso Fragoso ordered
olonel Pinheiro – acting commander of 4th Division – to concentrate
s forces in Juiz de Fora, just north of Rio de Janeiro, and then advance
n the Central Station, while another detachment would march from
res Coraçoes-Ijatubá on Mogi Mirim, and attack São Paulo from the
orth. However, in the early hours of 10 July, Pinheiro was replaced
y General Firmino Borba – who sympathised with the Paulistas and
as only waiting for his opportunity to take 4th Infantry Division to
e side of the rebels.

At 14:30hrs, Tasso Fragoso reiterated the orders for advances on
Mogi Mirim, Jacutinga and then to Campinas, north of the rebel
apital. This was a sound decision of strategic importance, for already
n the first day of the war the top general of the Brazilian Army had
orrectly defined the crucial points for the following battle. However,
orba ordered all of his forces to stop, and some even to withdraw
ack to Juiz de Fora. Instead, he called for a conference of all of the
ommanders of his units. At this meeting, Borba openly suggested
hat they switch sides. However, Major Penedo Pedra, a battalion
ommander, replied that he had never rebelled in 30 years of national
ervice, and saw no reason to do so now. His courageous words
onvinced the others. The result of this conference was that Borba was
rrested and jailed, and the command of 4th Division was returned to
Colonel Pinehiro.[16]

This was the crucial moment of the conflict, for had Borba managed
o bring at least a better part of 4th Division to the rebel side, he could
ave quickly ordered an advance on the capital and an end to Vargas's
ule before the war really began.

While this drama was developing in the rear of Minas, another
drama was in development at the HQ of 4th RCD in Tres Coraçoes.
There, the Paulista Colonel Andrade challenged the commander of
his unit, Colonel Eurico Gaspar Dutra (a future president of Brazil),
o prove his affiliation with the rebellion by securing the Mantiqueira
Tunnel. Dutra responded with the – rather generic – 'I will go there'.
However, instead of securing the tunnel, he redeployed 4th RCD
between 8th RAM and 4th BE, in turn annulling all of the Paulista
attempts to subvert these two units. Once he secured the loyalty of
he neighbouring units, Dutra then advanced on the tunnel, in turn
causing panic among the Paulistas.[17]

The final issue in these critical first few hours and then days of the
war was that of the southern and western borders of São Paulo State
and its allies. In order to secure these areas, Tasso Fragoso ordered the
troops of 3rd RM – nearly all of 3rd Infantry Division and including
three of the four regiments of 3rd Cavalry Division, and one from
1st Cavalry Division and other from 2nd Cavalry Division – and the
Military Brigade of Rio Grande do Sul to redeploy by sea to Paraná
in the south. Once there, these units would join with half of the 5th
Division to begin the operations. Finally, half of the troops of Mato
Grosso's Mixed Brigade would march against Campo Grande, home
of the revolt in the south part of Mato Grosso. [18]

What about the Paulistas' Allies?
The crucial state that the Paulistas expected to side with them was Rio
Grande do Sul. Positioned in the extreme south of Brazil, and home
to half of the Federal Army, this state also operated the most powerful
FP in the entire federation – and its FP units were all controlled by the
famous Military Brigade. Indeed, the governor of Rio Grande do Sul,
General Flores da Cunha, became involved in the revolt after former

Rio Grande do Sul governor, and Vargas' friend, Flores da Cunha,
standing up, and below, sitting down, ex-Riograndense President and
rebel Borges de Medeiros. (Diários Associados, São Paulo; via Donato

Rio Grande do Sul governor Flores da Cunha. (Drawing
by Belmonte. Folha de São Paulo, via Donato)

governor Borges de Medeirros requested him to do so in a telegraph
sent on 9 July 1932. However, da Cunha – while supporting the idea
of reconstitution – was also a personal friend of Vargas, who owed
him his position as governor of Gaúcho State. Thus, although initially
siding with the Paulistas, just a few hours later – at 01:20hrs on 10
July – da Cunha saved both his and Vargas's honour by submitting his
official resignation. With this, the position of the state of Rio Grande
do Sul was literally 'hanging in the air' for several hours. However,

A drawing of President Getúlio Vargas and his main military advisor and commander of the Army Detachment of the East, General Góis Monteiro. (Folha de São Paulo, via Donato)

Vargas quickly realised what was going on and arrived at the right decision: he decided to ignore his friend's resignation. At 01:35hrs, he answered from the Catete Palace with an appeal for da Cunha to keep their friendship in mind: 'I hope for the highest loyal and courageous attitude from my noble friend, in assuming control over Rio Grande.' Five minutes later, Vargas sent another message, insisting: 'I have your word that you will maintain order. I cannot accept your resignation. No one better than my dear friend could be the guarantor of the honour of Rio Grande … I am not going to give up … I am ready to die if necessary … A warm hug.'

Moreover, by 09:00hrs, Vargas – upon receiving further reports about the mutiny within the military and revolt on the streets – took out his revolver and wrote a manifesto stating that he would commit suicide if defeated. Moved by the fiery appeals and the possible death of his friend, da Cunha gave up. He wrote back: 'I will keep order or die.' With this, the fate of the Paulista uprising, and thus São Paulo State, was sealed.[19]

10–12 July 1932: The Birth of the Federal Mixed Aviation Group

On 10 July 1932, at the Dos Afonsos airfield, the Federals established the Mixed Aviation Group. Initially, this consisted of 13 aircraft, mostly drawn from the Military Aviation School: it included an Amiot 122 BP3 (K-621), two NiD-72 fighters (K-422 and K-423), six Potezs (A-114, A-115, A-117, A-211, A-216 and A-217) and four Wacos (C-1, C-3, C-4 and M), organised into two flights.[20] The Federals also had six DH.60 Moths, useful for liaison and reconnaissance purposes.[21]

With this equipment, General Góis Monteiro, who was very interested in the use of the air force, immediately issued the first orders on 10 July, stating that three fighter aircraft were always to be ready to intervene at the aerodrome of Dos Afonsos. At the same time, he ordered a large number of reconnaissance flights to locate the Paulista forces and determine whether or not they were advancing against Rio.

In comparison, the rebels only had four combat aircraft, half of them unarmed. Nevertheless, it was they who flew the first sorties of the war: on 10 July 1932, at 04:00hrs, a Fleet piloted by Lieutenant Joâo Silvio Hoeltz took off towards Campo Grande to take General Klinger to São Paulo. While making a stop in Baurú, the Fleet suffered heavy damage to its landing gear, and the general had to wait.[22] Shortly after, the Paulistas deployed the Waco 225 under Captain Ismael Torres Guilherme Christiano to drop propaganda leaflets over Rio. This sortie caused quite some consternation amongst the Federals –

A view of the massive and beautiful Martinelli Building in São Paulo. Anti-aircraft machine guns were deployed on its roof. (Daróz)

The little white dots visible in this photograph are Federal propaganda leaflets being dropped over São Paulo. (Daróz)

and especially for Góis Monteiro – who were surprised by the boldness of the rebels and their own inability to prevent such incursions.

Later during the day, the rebels launched their first combat air patrol over São Paulo, formed by the two precariously armed Wacos and the old Nieuport Ni 80.[23] Góis reacted immediately by organising a scouting mission along the Rio–São Paulo Railway with the Potez A-211, which, escorted by a Navy Corsair, also dropped propaganda leaflets over the rebel capital. Although rebel aircraft were airborne, the Federals were not intercepted.[24] Instead, São Paulo's answer was to install anti-aircraft guns on the roof of the Martinelli Building to protect the airspace of the city.[25]

On the next day, 11 July, Góis qualified his previous order, stating now that instead of three aircraft, at least one – but loaded with bombs – had to be ready to intervene at any time based on the results of aerial reconnaissance. At the same time, he sent three aircraft on a reconnaissance of the Taubaté area, to see if and where the advancing rebels were. On 12 July, aerial reconnaissance was extended to Cachoeira, and the mission was flown by Lieutenant Adil Joâo of Oliveira. On the same day, the Federals began installing machine guns into the front seats of Wacos C-1, C-3 and C-4 and shackles for

A rebel officer demonstrating a Hotchkiss machine gun, locally adapted as an anti-aircraft weapon. (Daróz)

General Góis Monteiro wearing a white summer uniform, probably from the Air Force, where he spent part of his military career. (Diários Associados, via Donato)

General Bertoldo Klinger, in the uniform, Commander-in-Chief of the Paulista forces, arriving at São Paulo by train alone, without any troops. Governor Pedro de Toledo is on the right. (Jorge Mancini, via Donato)

troops of the Mixed Brigade.[26]

13–14 July: The First Air Combat in America

On 13 July 1932, Góis ordered two aircraft to explore the area of Queluz-Jataí and Cachoeira. Lauvanére-Wanderley's Potez, with Homer Souto as observer, took off at 13:30hrs. It flew over Areia and Queluz before bombing the trenches dug by the Paulistas in the Cachoeira area. The second aircraft, a Potez coded A-217, with First Lieutenant Jose Sampaio and observer Marcio Macedo de Sousa e Mello 'Maluco', took off an hour later, following the same route. Over Bananal they discovered the Waco C-5, and Melo 'Maluco' (a future Minister of the Brazilian Federal government) opened fire. However, the rebel aircraft was able to flee at high speed and low

small bombs. The day ended with little consolation for the rebels, for even though General Klinger finally arrived in São Paulo from Mato Grosso, he did so by train, alone, and without the promised 5,000

altitude towards the south, because the Potez's machine gun jammed after only the first few bursts. Thus ended what was probably the first air combat ever fought over the South American continent – still

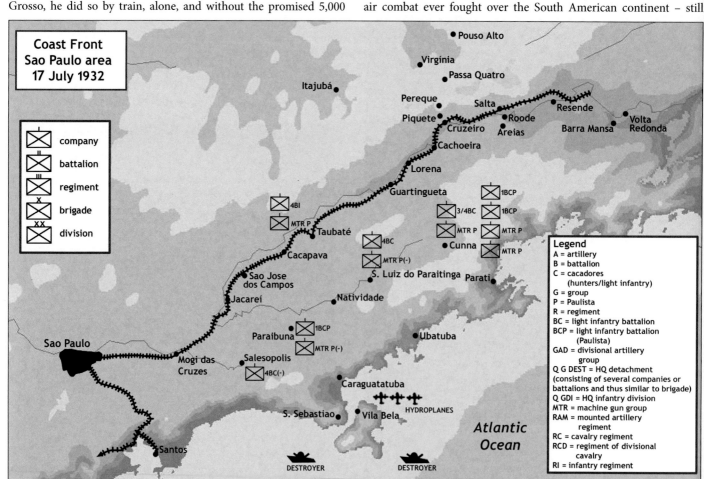

Based on Ramos, this map depicts the deployment of the Paulista Detachment Veiga Abreu on the Coastal Front as of 17 July 1932. Notable is the main concentration of units in the Cunha area, where they fought two battles and won two – rare – victories for the Paulistas. Note that the machine-gun units (MTR) shown were actually sections, not companies. (Map by Tom Cooper)

wo months before those of the
Chaco War.[27]

The first bombing sortie
f any city in Latin America
ollowed shortly later. This took
lace when the Potez A-217,
ccompanied by A-211, dropped
4 bombs on the troops of 4th
RI in Cachoeira. While the
recise details of results of this
ttack remain obscure, one
hing is sure: from what his
ilots reported, Góis Monteiro
vas able to deduct that the
aulistas had not advanced on
Rio. Therefore, there was little
or him to worry about: indeed,
e could focus on developing
is own plan for an offensive –
ncluding a strategic bombing
f São Paulo's industry. The
atter idea was objected to by his
Chief-of-Staff, Tasso Fragoso,
nd thus ruled out, at least for
he time being.[28]

On 14 July 1932, the Paulista
viation received a major boost
vhen First Lieutenant Arthur
la Motta Lima Filho flew in the
Waco C-3. This defection proved

Paulista volunteer troops arriving in São Paulo from the interior. Note their white handkerchiefs, that they still had not been armed, and do not wear any kind of helmet. (Coleção Paulo Florençano, Taubaté, via Donato)

anything other than easy. After taking off from Dos Afonsos, Lima
Filho was pursued by First Lieutenant Antonio Carlos da Silva Murici,
but the latter gave up when reaching Bananal. Shortly after, Lima Filho
came under attack by one of the Moths: the pilot evaded the fire and
then quickly landed in Taubaté – followed by the assailant, the pilot
of which, Captain Ismael Torres Guilherme Christiano, expressed his
surprise that his target was 'friendly'. The two agreed to a ceasefire
and decided to go to São Paulo to report their situation and have
somebody pick up their aircraft.[29]

The attack, with the Moth's speed of 135km/h and improvised gun
against the 210km/h and two synchronised machine guns of the Waco,
was almost suicidal and speaks much about the courage of Captain
Christiano. His decision was probably based on having an altitude
advantage, allowing him to gain speed in a surprise swoop against his
target. Lima Filho's Waco was probably the C-3 subsequently painted
in green that become known as the *Waco Verde*. It was to see much
more service than the other Paulista Wacos.

5

THE PARAÍBA VALLEY FRONT

As described above, the delay in the Paulista offensive against
the capital was vital for the government to buy time, mobilise
and deploy forces into blocking positions in front of Rio de Janeiro.
Sandwiched between the mountains of Sierra de Mantiqueira, inland
to the north, and the Sierra del Mar, parallel to the coast to the south,
there were only two ways to penetrate Rio: the Central Railroad of
Brazil (EFCB) and, slightly south, the highway that runs parallel to the
railway until it separates to the south-east in Areias. To protect these
points of access, in mid-July 1932 General Góis Monteiro organised

and deployed four 'detachments' along the border between the two
crucial states.

Deployment in the Valley

On his right – or northern – flank, Góis Monteiro deployed the
Detachment of Colonel Daltro Filho, composed mainly of 3rd RI
(about 1,500 officers and other ranks), positioned along the railway
near Engheneiro Passos. Further south, he deployed the Detachment
of Colonel Cristóvão Ferreira, with 1st RI (another 1,500 troops).
Along the Rio–São Paulo highway, Góis Monteiro brought into
position the Detachment Guedes Fontoura, with 2nd RI (again about
1,500 strong) in São José do Barreiro. Finally, in the extreme south,
on his left flank, was the Detachment Colonel Colatino Marques, with
the 500-strong 1st BC. Covering this deployment was the vanguard
consisting of 1st RCD (with some 500 cavalry in total). Even if never
specifically mentioned, these units were all reinforced with artillery:
in total, 1st and 2nd RAM had between 1,500 and 2,000 troops with
48 artillery pieces. These were deployed in several groups assigned to
each of the detachments. Nearly all of these 7,500 troops were from 1st
Infantry Division, which – at least officially – had a nominal strength
of 9,067 officers and other ranks as of 16 July.[1] This front line was then
reinforced by another 1,500 troops from 2nd and 3rd BC, and 1st BE,
additional elements of the BC, FP police and provisional battalions
from other parts of Brazil.[2] Moreover, in the Sierra de Mantiqueira,
Góis Monteiro formed the Southern Mineira Brigade, bringing
together elements of 4th Infantry Division and the Mineira FP. Its
task was to defend the approaches to Minas Gerais and threaten the
Paulista flank in the Paraíba Valley. Finally, between 21 and 22 July the
Army Detachment of the East would be created, bringing together all
these forces of 1st and 4th Divisions – the latter in Minas – under the
command of Góis Monteiro.[3]

Table 4: Ground Forces deployed in the Paraíba Valley as of 20 July 1932			
Federals: (General Goes Monteiro)	**East Army Detachment: 1st Division**		
Area	**Detachment**	**Units**	**Strength**
Right flank/northern flank: on the railway, at Engheneiro Passos	Daltro Filho	3rd RI	1,500
Centre-north	Ferreira	1st RI	1,500
Centre-south: São Paulo Highway, vs São João de Barreriro	Fontoura	2nd RI	1,500
Left/southern flank	Colatino Marques	1st BC	500
	Vanguard	1st RCI	500
Dispersed in all detachments	Artillery	1st RAM	750-1,000 & 24 guns
Dispersed in all detachments		2nd RAM	750-1,000 & 24 guns
Total			**7,000-7,500 Men & 48 Guns**
Paulistas:			
2nd Division in Operations: Col. Figueiredo.			
Left/northern flank: Cruzeiro, vs Tunnel de Mantiqueira	Sampaio	2 Companies, 1st and 2nd Battalion/5th RI	
		2 Companies, 5th BCP	
		3 Companies, 2nd BCP	
		1 battery, 2nd GIAP	
		1 battery, 2nd GAD	
Total			**1,300 & 8 cannons**
Forward, centre: Queluz, ECFB rail	Agnelo	2 Companies, 1st Battalion 5th RI	
		2 Companies, 1st BCPR	
		'Iberé' Volunteer Battalion	
Total			700
Right flank: Areias, Rio–São Paulo road	Andrade	1st Battalion/6th RI	
		1st Battalion/4th RI	
		1 Company of 2nd Battalion/4th RI	
		4 Companies of FPP	
		2 Squadrons of 2nd RCD	
		2 Batteries of 2nd GAD	
		1 flame-thrower vehicle	
Total			**1,800 men, 8 cannons**
Total in the front line			**3,800 men & 16 cannons**
Paulistas Reserves (under General Klinger's direct control)			
Reserve North: Guaratinguetá-Piquete	Abilio	2nd and 3rd Battalions/6th RI	
		1 volunteer battalion	
		2 Companies, 1st BCPR	
		1 artillery Section/2nd GAD	
Total			**1,550 & 2 cannons**
Reserve South: Coast	Veiga Abreu	3 Companies, 4th BC	
		3 Companies, 1st BCP	
Total			**600**
Total Reserves:			2,150 men & 2 cannons
TOTAL PAULISTAS:			5,950 men, 18 cannons, 1 flame-thrower

On the other side, the rebels meanwhile organised themselves into ve detachments. Detachment Sampaio, based in Cruzeiro, was slightly ɔ the rear and facing north, facing the Federalist troops threatening ɔ attack the Paulista defences from the rear. The unit included about ,300 combatants, including two companies of 1st and 2nd Battalions ɔf 5th RI, two companies of 5th BCP, three companies from 2nd BCP, ɪne battery of 2nd GIAP and another battery from 2nd GAD.

Facing east was the Detachment Major Agnelo, based in Queluz, ɪn the ECFB railway. This counted only about 700 troops from two ɔmpanies of 1st Battalion of 5th RI, two companies from 1st BCPR ɪnd the *Ibere* Volunteer Battalion. To the right of the Detachment Major Agnelo was the Detachment Colonel Andrade, based in ʌreias, on the road connecting Rio with São Paulo. This was about ,800-strong, and included troops from 1st Battalion of 6th RI, 1st Battalion of 4th RI, one company from 2nd Battalion 4th RI, four ɔmpanies of the FPP, two squadrons of 2nd RCD, two batteries of ₤nd GAD and one flame-thrower vehicle. Finally, the Detachment Colonel Abilio represented the reserve. Based in Guaratinguetá, ⱡhis comprised some 1,550 troops from 2nd and 3rd Battalions of ₤th RI, one volunteer battalion, two companies of 1st BCPR and an ɪrtillery section of 2nd GAD. Separated from Colonel Abilio was ⱡhe Detachment Veiga Abreu, tasked to defend the coast. This unit ɔonsisted of 600 troops from three companies of 4th BC and three ɔompanies of 1st BCP – all from 2nd Infantry Division, commanded ɔy Colonel Figueiredo. Overall, the Paulistas thus had about 5,950 ⱡroops in the Paraíba Valley by 20 July.[4]

Perhaps more importantly, out of the five Paulista detachments ⱡhat were present, just two – about 2,500 troops in total – were facing ɪn the direction of Rio, i.e. actually holding the main front. The rest ⱡvere protecting the flanks of the main front line. Unsurprisingly, ɪn this area, the Federalists enjoyed superiority of at least two-to-ɔne in detachments and three-to-one in troops. This superiority ⱡvas to continue growing as Góis Monteiro was able to send more ɾeinforcements to the front – and even more so because the Paulistas ⱡvere not only slow in exploiting the opportunity to advance on the capital, early on, but then also slow in evacuating their troops to the bottleneck in the Paraíba Valley and thus narrowing their front lines.

Settling down in their positions, the rebels next started construction ɔf a complex system of trenches, protected by barbed wire. They took ⱡadvantage of numerous hills amongst the coffee plantations, and also ɔoccupied all the dominant peaks in the nearby mountains. This was ɪntended to cause any Federal offensive to advance very slowly and ‖suffer extensive losses while trying to break through the main front ‖ine – even with extensive support from artillery and aviation.

13–15 July 1932: Areias and São José Do Barreiro

As mentioned above, the Paulista front line in the sector between Areias and São José do Barreiro, along the road connecting Rio with ‖São Paulo, was held by the Detachment Colonel Andrade. This unit ⱡvas reasonably well-deployed, with 1st Battalion of 6th RI, half of 1st Battalion of 4th RI, two FPP companies and an artillery battery (with four pieces) from 2nd GAD entrenched about 1.5km north of Barreiro. Behind them, and covering the left flank, was a company from 2nd Battalion of 4th RI, one FPP company, a section of heavy machine guns from 6th RI, a platoon from 2nd RCD and a section of mounted ⱡartillery (two pieces). A company of 4th RI, another company of the FPP, half a platoon from 2nd RCD, a section of heavy machine guns from 6th RI, a section of mounted artillery (two pieces) and a flame-thrower vehicle were at the Fazenda Santa Rita. Half a company from ‖4th RI and half a platoon from 2nd RCD held the Fazenda Palmares, while the detachment's reserve consisted of two companies from 1st

Battalion of 4th RI, three heavy machine-gun sections, a company from 6th RI and a squadron from 2nd RCD, based in Areias.[5]

Over the following days, this significant concentration was progressively reinforced by 5th BCPM (two companies of 5th BCP, one emergency company made up from volunteers and two sections of machine guns), and then two companies of 1st BCP. The first Federalist offensive was to hit precisely the latter troops, who held the southernmost Paulista positions in the Paraíba Valley.

14–15 July 1932: Federal Aviation in the Valley

After making sure that the Paulistas were not advancing on Rio, Góis Monterio ordered his aviation into repeated attacks on the newly discovered airfield in Taubaté, with the intention of destroying the rebel aviation on the ground and thus securing aerial superiority. Theoretically, the Paulistas had five aircraft deployed at this base, but these operated ineffectively. Encouraged, Góis thus ordered his sole Amiot to drop a load of leaflets over São Paulo on 15 July. This mission was aborted due to an engine failure. However, not informed of the cancellation, the fighter supposed to fly top cover flew its part of the mission and the Waco M piloted by Lieutenant Carlos da Silva Murici appeared all alone over São Paulo. While passing above Taubaté, he encountered a lone DH.60 Moth, attacked it and forced it to land. On the way back from his mission, da Silva Murici then strafed his opponent on the ground.[6]

Later during the day, and because the naval base at Ilhabela was still incomplete, the Naval Aviation provided four of its Corsairs (1-0-2, 1-0-3, 1-0-4 and 1-0-6) led by Lieutenant Commander D'jalma Petit to the Army, which in turn sent them into reconnaissance sorties over the Paraíba Valley.[7]

15–28 July 1932: Emergence of the Paulista Air Force

Through all of this time, the Paulista aviation hardly ever tried to oppose the Federalists.[8] The primary reason was not just that only two Wacos were – partially – armed, but also the lack of experienced pilots. All of the available fliers were actually civilians, and their commander – Major Torres Guillermino Christiano – was a medical doctor who acquired his flying licence for his love of aircraft. Indeed, even his deputy, Capitain João Negrão, was a civilian firefighter. Not only the first commander of the Fighter Squadron (which operated no fighters at all) – Sebastão Machado – but also other members of what was actually just a flight, such as Reynaldo Gonçalves and Alberto Americano, were all civilians. The most experienced amongst them was Machado Bittencourt, who had recently escaped from Rio.[9]

After the defection of Waco C-3 on 14 July, piloted by Lieutenant Arthur Lima da Motta Filho, there were still only three pilots with military experience. It was only on 19 July that the Paulistas were reinforced by First Lieutenants Orsini de Araújo Coriolano and José Angelo Gomes, and on 25 July by Major Ivo Borges and Major Lysias Rodriguez (both of whom arrived on a fishing boat). With Borges being the most experienced flier around, he took over as the commander of what was officially designated the Constitutionalist Air Unit (UAC) on 28 July. A day later, Rodriguez was appointed as commander of the 1st Fighter Aviation Group (1 GAvCA). The latter was subdivided into two flights: the attack element was commanded by Captain Ismael Torres Guilherme Christiano, and the reconnaissance flight by First Lieutenant José Ángelo Gomes Ribeiro. Despite related planning, the third unit – the Mixed Aviation Group – never came into being, due to the lack of necessary aircraft and pilots.[10]

The UAC was constantly experiencing every imaginable problem related to its equipment. According to a Paulista prisoner interrogated on 20 July, the Wacos still had no machine guns to fire forwards, but an

Major Ivo Borges. After reaching the Paulista lines by escaping from Rio in a fishing boat, he assumed command of the Constitutionalist Air Unit (UAC). (Daróz)

Major Lysias Rodrigues also escaped from Rio with Borges and was appointed commander of the rebel 1st Fighter Aviation Group. (Daróz)

Major Eduardo Gomes, supreme commander of the Federal Mixed Group, operating mainly in the Paraíba Valley. He later moved to Pouso Alegre to organise the Minas Air Detachment. (Daróz)

observer located in the rear cockpit was equipped with a sub-machine gun and could fire towards the side and the rear.[11] Unsurprisingly, the Waco C-3 and the Potezs became the favourite aircraft of the Paulistas, while other machines were used for secondary purposes only. That said, this early during the war the Federal aviation was also experiencing problems: for example, machine guns on Wacos tended to jam because the ammunition provided to them was drawn from infantry stocks and had a larger calibre than necessary. Ultimately, they all ended up being used almost exclusively as bombers, equipped with A-3 racks or other 'portable' weapons carried by their pilots.[12]

Regardless of the issues with their armament, pending the imminent offensive, on 16 July all the operational aircraft were ordered into air strikes on two Paulista airfields: Campo de Marte in São Paulo and Taubaté in the Paraíba Valley. The commander of the Federal Mixed Group, Major Eduardo Gomes, went on to direct the operation flying as an observer in the aircraft piloted by Nelson Lavandére-Wanderley. This was escorted by one Vought O2U-2A Navy Corsair at high altitude (flown by Djalma Petit), a Waco registered as C-1 or C-4, three Potez TOEs (A-211, A-216 and A-217) and the sole Amiot 122 (K-621).[13] These six aircraft appeared over São Paulo at 13:30hrs, to release 40 bombs on Campo de Marte, and then leaflets over the city. Later the same day, a sole Potez (A-115) also attacked Taubaté.[14]

Both airstrikes proved ineffective: indeed, they failed to hit even one of the Paulista aircraft on the ground as the rebels had meanwhile redeployed the entire UAV to Itapetininga airfield, in the south, where these were deployed to compensate for the shortage of troops and artillery. Thus, the Federalists achieved air superiority despite ineffective air strikes, and their engineers began constructing a new airfield outside Resende, close to the border with São

Paulista Wacos C-2 and C-5 (behind). Note that these aircraft were painted in the same red as the Federal *vermelinhos*, and so to differentiate them a black-white-black line was painted on the lower wing. (Daróz)

aulo. This became operational during the second half of July.[15]

Table 5: Combat Aircraft in the Paraíba Valley as of 10 July 1932

Federals

	Mixed Aviation Group (Dos Afonsos):		
Type	Plate	Main role	Notes
Amiot 122	K-621	Bomber	
NiD.72	K-423	Fighter	
NiD.72	K-422	Fighter	
Potez	A-114	Bomber	
Potez	A-115	Bomber	
Potez	A-117	Bomber	
Potez	A-211	Bomber	
Potez	A-216	Bomber	
Potez	A-217	Bomber	
Waco	C-1	Fighter-Bomber	Armed with kit
Waco	C-3	Fighter-Bomber	Armed with kit. Defected on 14 July
Waco	C-4	Fighter-Bomber	Armed with kit
Waco	'M'	Fighter-Bomber	Originally armed
Naval Aviation (Ilabelha)			
Corsair	1-0-2	Fighter	
Corsair	1-0-3	Fighter	
Corsair	1-0-4	Fighter	
Corsair	1-0-6	Fighter	

Paulista

Waco	C-2	Bomber	Improvised armed
Waco	C-3	Fighter-Bomber	Obtained from the Federals on 14 July, properly armed (*Waco Verde*)
Waco	C-5	Bomber	Improvised armed
Potez	A-116	Fighter-Bomber	
Potez	A-212	Fighter-Bomber	

17–22 July 1932: Air Strikes on São José Do Barreiro

With the skies in the theatre dominated, on 17 July the first timid Federal advance began, made by the 2nd RI of Detachment Fontoura, from Santana dos Tocos in Rio de Janeiro State, that could threaten Areias from the north-east, or intercept the route to São José do Barreiros, a village that was in a wedge, a little further south.[16] In this salient was Captain Odilon Company, 5th BCP, which, seeing their rear threatened, received reinforcement from elements of 4th RI, 6th RI, 2nd RCD and an artillery battery, troops sent from the Mantiqueira Tunnel, all under Major Quintiliano. With these reinforcements, the 17 July attack was repulsed.

Weather conditions prevented the Varguistas from enjoying air support in the south, although apparently these did not preclude new missions further north: on the morning of the 17th, a Federal aircraft discovered that Taubaté was deserted, so the attack was later launched against Campo de Marte, São Paulo, with four aircraft, the Amiot K-621 and three Potezs, that dropped 38 bombs, but the attack missed its target.[17] Finally, on 19 July, the weather improved in the southern sector, and on this date the Potezs A-211 and 216 attacked the Paulista

Paulista soldiers, wearing Adrian 1915 steel helmets, operating a locally manufactured anti-aircraft machine gun at Cruzeiro railway station. This may be the one that damaged Potez A-211. (Daróz)

artillery at São José do Barreiro, dropping 12 bombs. Góis Monteiro's very detailed plan, that aircraft would attack the front lines, then the trenches of the second line and finally the artillery, was followed successfully. At the same time the infantry would also open fire, but not the artillery, so as not to risk their own aircraft. The troops would then launch an assault to take advantage of the chaos caused by the bombing. One of the aircraft, according to pilot-observer Montezuma, bombed the rebel artillery from only 200 metres altitude. On the 20th, the Federal Mixed Group made another attack flying at ground level and, adding up to six aircraft (Potezs A-211, A-117 and A-217, and Wacos C-1, C-4 and 'M'), crushed the Paulista battery at São João, depriving the rebels of artillery support in the sector, which would prove vital to the subsequent government victory. That day, another bombing of a train by an aircraft, missed its target.[18]

On the land front, on 21 July Captain Carvalho executed a counter-attack against Santana dos Tocos with two squadrons of 2nd RCD, six FPP battle groups and a machine-gun company that was violently repulsed when he was faced by 2nd RI and 1st Federal RCD. In this clash there were only about 900 Paulistas against some 2,000 government troops.[19]

Furthermore, air strikes continued, and on the 21st and 22nd positions at Queluz, Taubaté (by two aircraft) and São José do Barreiro were again bombarded, destroying an artillery battery from 4th RAM. Lorena airfield was also attacked. A Federal aircraft surprised a convoy between Queluz and Taubaté but did not attack it as it moved into locations occupied by civilians. In the sectors of Cruzeiro and the tunnel, on 22 July, Lieutenant Americo dos Reis, flying over the 1,800-metre-high Sierra de Mantiqueira, reported that neither the speedometer, altimeter nor the gasoline indicator of his Potez A-211 were showing a correct reading. To make matters worse, the gunner-observer position had been struck by fire from Túnel and Piquete, nearly wounding the co-pilot. Lintz Geraldo also mentioned, at some unspecified time around 22 August, that a Federal Potez 106 was destroyed over Guaratinguetá, perhaps by rebel anti-aircraft artillery. No Potez matches this description, while a Corsair lost by accident on 20 August with number 1-0-6 or 106 was operating in the south.[20]

20–29 July 1932: Offensive on Barreiro

On 23 July, Góis Monteiro ordered a massive new attack by all operational Federal aircraft. The Mixed Group reached a total of 10 aircraft under Eduardo Gomes, including two Corsair naval aircraft under Petit. All of these aircraft bombed Campo de Marte again, dropping 69 bombs that damaged the airfield hangar, but caused no major damage. A bomb was dropped by mistake near the Club Esperia,

Government Waco C-4, armed with the machine gun kit, and Potez A-117 preparing for a mission. Potez A-117 was the first aircraft downed in air-to-air combat in the Western Hemisphere, on 8 August, a month before the famous shooting down in the Chaco War. (Oscar Xavier de Fraga)

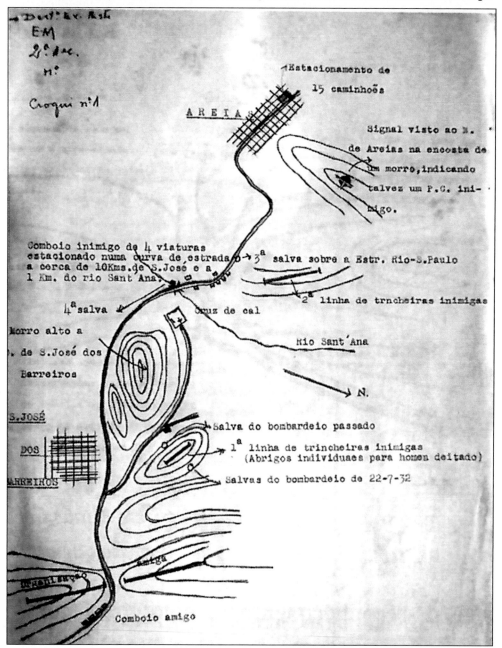

A sketch drawn by the Federal aviation after the bombing of the battery of São José do Barreiro. Slightly below the centre, the bombing of 22 July is also shown. (Daróz)

which was full of children and women, causing panic in São Paulo. Taubaté was also attacked. According to some sources Brazilian 55kg (120lb) F bomb were used for the first time however, surviving pictures show what appear to be standard 11kg (25lb) A Type bombs. No details are recorded of which aircraft were involved, but there were probably two or three Wacos (C-1, C-4 and 'M'), the five or six identified Potezs (114, 115, 117, 211, 216 and 218) and the two Corsairs. Nevertheless, there are doubts about whether this number was really put in the air, as Góis Monteiro recalled that the maximum number of aircraft used in a single mission was seven. On 22 and 23 July, the Federal aviation also attempted to destroy the Cachoeira Paulista bridge, which would have left the rebels split by the Paraíba river. Due to bad weather from 24–27 July, only liaison, reconnaissance, propaganda and artillery correction missions could be flown. On 25 July, the Federal aircraft dropped a crown of flowers into São Paulo as a tribute to Santos Dumont, Brazilian aviation pioneer and aircraft inventor, who had committed suicide as he saw with horror how his creation was being used to kill other Brazilians. Later, Potez A-211 left for the southern front on 26 July, to provide some air cover in this sector where all of the São Paulo aviation was concentrated.[21]

Aviation made a very important, though less dramatic, contribution to the government's general offensive which began on 27 July, through missions such as artillery observation. This coincided with the displacement of the Federal Mixed Group from Campo dos Afonsos to Resende, to bring it closer to the front and avoid crossing the Sierra de Mantiqueira on the outward and return journeys, with the corresponding risk of air accidents. To this end, the Resende Air Detachment was created. The first pilots assigned to this detachment would be First Lieutenants Araripe Macedo, Lavanére-Wanderley and Americo dos Reis. During the war, this detachment would be directed first by Araripe, later by Murici Filho, and finally by Captain Americo dos Reis.[22] At the same time, one of the Corsairs departed from the naval airbase at Galeão to join the

DEST.EX.DE LESTE   Q.G.em Barra Mansa,22 de Julho de 1932

DIV.DO VALE DO
PARAIBA

Estado Maior

3a. Secç-ão

Nº 59

(URGENTE)

     ORDEM PARTICULAR 'Nº 35

     (Missões da Aviação no dia 23)

I - A aviação fará amanhã sobre S.PAULO uma demonstração de força:
     1)-fazendo voar o maior numero de aviões que for possivel;
     2)-bombardeando a baixa altura,aviões e hangares no Campo de Mar
     te.

II - O fim visado é abater o moral dos revoltosos.

II - No regresso ás nossas linhas, si dispuserem ainda de bombas,bom-
bardear aviões e hangares nos campos:

     TAUBATÉ
     CACHOEIRA
     CRUZEIRO

        Jen. Góy

Destinatarios:

Chefe   - E.M.E.

Diretor da Av.Mil.

Cmt. Grupo da Av.

2a.Secção

Góis Monteiro's order, dated 22 July, to bomb Campo de Marte, São Paulo, 'with the maximum number of available planes', at 'low level', and to also then attack Taubaté, Cachoeira and Cruzeiro on the return. (Daróz)

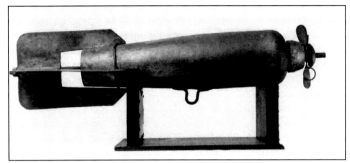

Detailed view of the 11kg (25lb) A type bomb used by the Federals in the 23 July Campo de Marte bombing. This appears to be the same as the bombs shown in the photograph below. (Daróz)

Resende Detachment, along with another Corsair previously intended for the Paraíba Valley. That same day, the Federal Potez A-216 piloted by Faria Lima crashed and damaged its landing gear.[23] Nevertheless, it seems that this was not a total loss, and was repaired.

On 28 July the Federals launched airstrikes again, although pilot Américo dos Reis was not able to find the Paulista artillery and instead bombed a train with eight wagons near Areias. The next day, 29 July, after 48 hours of artillery bombardment, 2nd RI from Detachment Fontoura managed to break the Paulista defences, pushing back 4th RI and 2nd Company/5th BCPM, enveloping São José do Barreiros from the north and taking the position of Morro Pelado. Andrade gave the order to retreat the whole detachment to the town of Areias, in the Morro do Frio, in order to avoid the risk of being surrounded. During the offensive, a large number of Paulistas were captured; terrified of aerial bombardment, they had abandoned their positions and weapons in order to save themselves. The battle of Barreiros was probably the first sustained air campaign to support a land offensive in the Americas.[24]

That same day, 29 July, Federal Waco C-1, piloted by Lieutenant Antonio Carlos da Silva Murici, carried out a mission to drop propaganda and was attacked in error by Federal Potez A-117, flown by Joelmir Araripe Macedo, near Tunnel de Mantiqueira, only being saved by a sharp turn.[25]

27 July – 3 August: Battle of Salto

While all of this was happening in the southern part of the Paraíba Valley, in the centre, where the EFCB railroad ran, a government assault was launched. Góis Monteiro was skilfully alternating attacks in the northern and southern sectors in order to force the Paulistas to retire troops to cover the sector being attacked, and then attacking the newly weakened sector.

Since 10 July, the Salto bridge over the EFCB and Paraíba river, east of Queluz, had been protected by a patrol of the Paulista 5th RI. Along with the reinforcements arriving over successive days, Detachment Agnelo was formed. On 20 July, this was deployed as follows: a company from 1st Battalion/5th RI, at Queluz with about 100

Rebel soldiers in Campo de Marte show what appear to be unexploded 11kg (25lb) A type bombs used by the Federals in the 23 July attack rather than the heavier 55kg (120lb) F type bombs claimed to have been used by the Federals for the first time during this bombing. (Daróz)

soldiers; another company of 1st Battalion/5th RI, two companies of 1st BCPR and 'Iberê' Battalion in Salto, adding about 700 soldiers.[26]

A mountain artillery battery from Detachment Sampaio, that was watching to the north in the rear of the Sierra de Mantiqueira, arrived on 18 July; a heavy artillery battery and a company from 'Escola' Battalion on the 19th; 165 soldiers of 'Baia' Battalion on the 22nd; a company of 'Abilio' Battalion from Rezende on the 25th; and some 30 Fire Brigade men and 45 from 'Piracicabano' Battalion on the 26th. With such inexpert and heterogeneous troops, a disaster was inevitable.[27]

With all these being fragments of other units, the supply of arms, ammunition and food was a nightmare, as the headquarters of the unit often did not even know exactly where these small groups were placed. Despite this chaos, some patrols were able to cross the Rio de Janeiro State, take Engenheiro Passos rail station and move forward almost to Itatiaia.[28] Units of the 8th BCR and the Santos Civic Militia were also involved in this sector.[29] In the meantime, the Federal Detachment Daltro Filho concentrated its forces to expel them, and from 14 July, 3rd RI maintained contact with the Paulistas. This unit moved by train from Resende to Itaíaia, and its vanguard to Engenheiro Passos. However, the Paulista artillery and a night attack forced them to retreat back to Resende on the 18th. Nevertheless, on 20 July they returned and managed to retake the station.[30] On 21 and 22 July, as we have seen, the government aircraft bombed the Paulista positions and artillery in Queluz, and after a week of preparation and threatening to engulf rebel positions in Moraes, Facenda Garcez and Nelo Puccini, Monteiro finally launched the great general offensive on the 27th, coinciding with the attack over São José do Barreiro. On 30 July, Lieutenant Americo dos Reis's aircraft attacked trucks on the Rio–São Paulo highway, and Francisco Melo's aircraft dropped 12 bombs on a group of vehicles in Cachoeira. By early August, Monteiro's Federal East Army Detachment had been greatly strengthened with temporary and police troops, and now totalled up to 18,300 men.[31]

Around Salto, after a bitter struggle, Detachment Ferreira, with the 1st RI, finally managed to take the Fazenda Palmeiras region. According to Donato, the Fazenda had been occupied by the Paulistas on 14 July by Captain Veloso, taking 32 prisoners. The next day, the government counter-attacked with 3rd RI, air support and artillery, but were repulsed, losing another 30 soldiers that were captured. On 16 July, the Paulistas' positions were again targeted by aircraft and artillery. Finally, on 27 July, the São Paulo aviation, according to Donato, mistakenly bombed the position, forcing the rebels to abandon Palmeiras, but considering that the Paulista aircraft had abandoned the front on the 16th, they were again probably Federal aircraft.[32] The Paulista Palmeiras position finally fell into the hands of 1st RI. Once covered with this operation, the left flank of Detachment Filho's 3rd RI finally broke the left flank of the Paulistas Detachment Agnelo on 2 August, taking the Salto bridge, on 3rd RI's left flank, the next day along with the disputed Bianor. The Paulistas' armoured train went to the Salto bridge to cover the rebels' withdrawal.[33]

3–5 August: Detachment Teófilo Replaces the Dissolved Agnelo

This disaster led to Lieutenant Colonel Teófilo Ramos being urgently called from the Tunnel of Mantiqueira on the same day to take command of the near-destroyed Paulista Agnelo Detachment in Queluz. The city was full of soldiers roaming the streets instead of being at the front line, refusing to obey orders and calling for their comrades to withdraw to safety. Improvising, Teófilo was able to gather 100 soldiers from '7 September' Battalion, who were sent to take positions on the left bank of the Paraíba, and a company of FPP

recruits, who occupied the right bank on the railroad, to reconstitute a line near Bianor on 5 August.[34] The Santos Tiro Naval troops also arrived.[35] The struggle for Bianor lasted several days. On 4 August protected by machine guns, Varguistas took the station, only to lose it in a Paulista counterattack. The next day, government troops retook the station before losing it again, the building eventually falling into their hands one more time. During the night, Colonel Figueiredo sent the Paulista armoured train, equipped with artillery and machine guns, from Queluz to Bianor, which caused panicked Federals to flee the station. However, due to lack of fresh troops, Figueiredo was not able to follow up this success, so the station was regained by government forces.[36]

With the Queluz disbandment, it became necessary to reform the entire Paulista Detachment. The terrified, defeatist troops and deserters were moved far from the front line, even as far as Cruzeiro and Lorena, to avoid their despairing attitude spreading to the other forces. Replacements arrived in the form of the Castro Cavalry Squadron of 5th RCD from Paraná State (one of the few units located in this region that joined the rebels, as we will see), 1st BCR from Santos (with 180 armed soldiers and 120 unarmed) and a machine gun section of 5th BFP. However, the defensive cordon around Queluz was so weak that it was considered necessary to retain the heavy artillery from the 2nd GIAP in the rearguard, still loaded on the train in Lavrinhas.[37]

Fortunately for the Paulistas, bad weather prevented the Federal aviation from launching major actions. Only two Potezs bombed Lorena airfield on 1 August, with little result, as all the rebel aircraft that should have been parked there were still on the South Front. The aircraft made two passes at 1,000 metres, but due to damage to one aircraft from ground fire, a second pass was made at up to 1,500 metres. Faria Lima and Adil de Oliveira reported observing three Paulista aircraft in the field, although perhaps they were civil and not combat aircraft. That same day, Lieutenant Geraldo Aquino attacked three trucks on the São Paulo–Rio road. The Federals were limited to reconnaissance missions on 3, 4, 7 and 8 August, with a single bombing mission made by Joaquim Lorena Libanios on the 8th.[38] On 5 August, a Federal Waco, despite the horrendous weather, dared to make a reconnaissance flight to Areias and Queluz, but ended up crash-landing and being destroyed. The destroyed plate number is not mentioned, but given that in the later stages of the conflict we have reports from only Wacos C-4 and 'M', the destroyed aircraft was probably C-1 with Lieutenants Botelho and Ballousier. With just a two-man crew, the Federal Waco had to fly defectively armed or even unarmed. It was perhaps the same aircraft that was intended for Góis Monteiro on a mission to locate the Paulista armoured train on the same date. Later, on 9 August, the Federal Potez of Lieutenant Araripe and observer Montezuma was hit by anti-aircraft artillery when bombing Silveira.[39]

6–8 August 1932: Fall of Bianor and Areias

As the struggle between Federals and Paulistas for Bianor continued, on 6 or 7 August the government forces captured an entire FPP machine-gun section that protected the Morro da Fortaleza. From there they strafed the Paulistas forces, and advanced again to Bianor, threatening to surround them and ejecting the '7 September' Battalion from the left bank of the Paraíba river. Despite being deprived of artillery, as we have said, Figueiredo ordered a counter-attack to regain the station: at dawn Detachment Andrade would attack the flank of Salto bridge from the south, recover the station, and isolate the Federal deployment in the Morro de Fortaleza, while on the Bianor front the Teófilo Detachment would attack to distract the Varguistas.

Six Potez 25 TOEs were deployed by the Federals as bombers. This one, registered as A-117, was the only one shot down in air combat during the Paulista War, and was also the first aircraft ever shot down in air combat in all of Latin America. Specifications of the Potez 25 TOE were: maximum speed 215km/h; manoeuvre ratio 0.14 (357kw engine, 2,558kg loaded weight); ceiling 5,500m; range 600km. Armament: 1 or 2 x Vickers 7.7mm machine guns forward; 2 x Darne 7.7mm machine guns rear; 240kg of bombs. (Artwork by Luca Canossa)

Including Waco CSOs, the Federals had 19 Waco 240 *vermelinho* fighter-bombers. This example (C-18) was used for artillery correction and reconnaissance operations in the Paraíba. Specifications: maximum speed 210km/h; manoeuvre ratio 0.19 (179kw engine, 920kg loaded weight); range 868km. Armament: 2 x MG-40 7mm machine guns forward; 140kg of bombs. (Artwork by Luca Canossa)

This is a reconstruction of one of two NiD.72s operated by the Federals. The K-422 participated in the destruction of the Paulista Potez A-116 on the ground. Specifications: maximum speed 260km/h; manoeuvre ratio 0.3 (447kw engine, 1,471kg loaded weight); ceiling 8,200m; range 400km. Armament: 2 x Vickers machine guns forward. (Artwork by Luca Canossa)

The Federals operated one or two Amiot 122 BP3s as bombers in the early stages of the war. This illustration shows the only example known to have been operational. Specifications: maximum speed 205km/h; manoeuvre ratio 0.11 (485kw engine, 4,500kg loaded weight); range 1,000km. Armament: Vickers 5 and Lewis 0.303/7.7mm machine guns (2 x forward, 2 x rear, 1 x ventral); 800kg of bombs. (Artwork by Luca Canossa)

Federal LeO-253Bn.4. This heavy bomber was not used due to lack of trained crews. Specifications: maximum speed 230km/h; manoeuvre ratio 0.1 (2 x 485kw engine, 9,560kg loaded weight); ceiling 8,000m; range 1,500km. Armament: 3 x 7.5mm machine guns; up to 800kg of bombs. (Artwork by Luca Canossa)

This was one of four Vought O2UA Corsairs operated by the Federals. It mainly operated in the coastal sector and then in the south. Specifications: maximum speed 260km/h; manoeuvre ratio 0.21 (447kw engine, 2,161kg loaded weight); ceiling 5,670m; range 1,094km. Armament: 2 x 7.62mm machine guns, one fore and the other aft; 226.5kg of bombs. (Artwork by Luca Canossa)

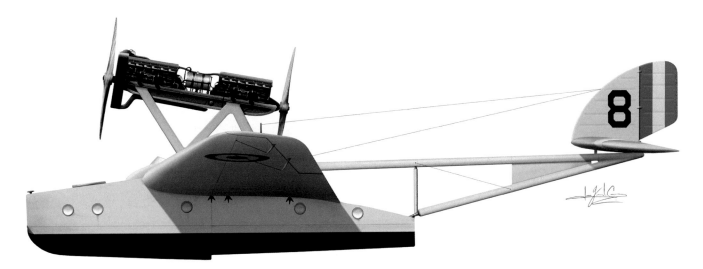

Federal Savoia-Marchetti SM.55A navy heavy bomber and recce. Six samples participated in the blockade and bombing of Santos, and it was part of the first strategic bombing in the Western Hemisphere. Specifications: maximum speed 280km/h; ceiling 5,000m; range 4,600km. Armament: 4 x Lewis machine guns (one in each of the two prows and sterns); 2,000kg of bombs. (Artwork by Luca Canossa)

This was one of two Martin PM-1s operated by the Federals. Both were used as naval bombers and for reconnaissance purposes. This one was sunk in a storm on 12 September after participating in the blockade and air raids over Santos, thus becoming part of the first campaign of strategic bombing in the Western Hemisphere. Specifications: maximum speed 184km/h; ceiling 3,300m; range 2,100km. Armament: 2 x Lewis 0.303 machine guns (one in the fore and aft); 416kg of bombs. (Artwork by Luca Canossa)

De Havilland DH-60T Moth used by the Federals for naval reconnaissance and liaison purposes along the coast in the Southern Front, mainly in the Rio Grande do Sul. A few of the Moths were equipped with machine guns, some with bombs and others simply with a radio. Specifications: maximum speed 164km/h; manoeuvre ratio 0.1 (75kw engine, 750kg loaded weight); ceiling 4,420m; range 510km. (Artwork by Luca Canossa)

This Avro 504 N/O was flown by the Federals for naval reconnaissance in Mato Grosso do Sul but saw no combat operations. Specifications: maximum speed 140km/h; manoeuvre ratio 0.09 (75kw engine, 830kg loaded weight); ceiling 4,875m; range 402km. Armament: 1 x Lewis .303 machine gun forward. (Artwork by Luca Canossa)

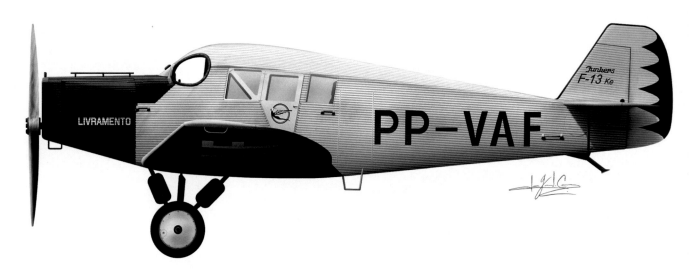

Federal Junkers F-13 navy reconnaissance aircraft owned by the Varig Company and requisitioned by the Navy. It is painted here with its civilian markings; the military ones are unknown. It operated in Mato Grosso do Sul, where it discovered the Paulista Bronze Column's march. Specifications: maximum speed 173km/h; ceiling 5,000m; range 1,400km. (Artwork by Luca Canossa)

The Paulistas attempted to hijack this privately owned Sikorsky S-38 transport in Rio de Janeiro. However, the aircraft crashed due to a fight between its crew members. Specifications: maximum speed 200km/h; ceiling 5,500m; range 966km. (Artwork by Luca Canossa)

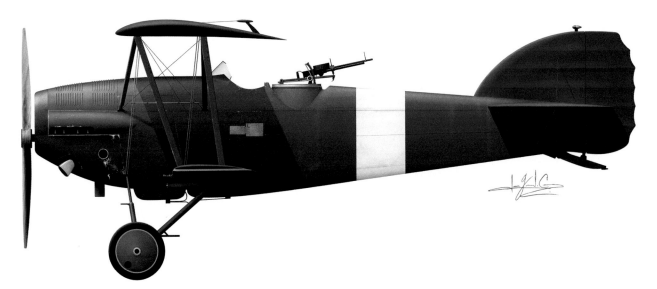

This is a reconstruction of one of two Potez 25 TOEs operated by the Paulistas. The aircraft became known as the '*Nosso Potez*' ('Our Potez') and shot down Federal Potez A-117 before crashing on 21 or 23 September. Its number plate A-212 was hidden under the Paulista white band. Specifications: maximum speed 215km/h; manoeuvre ratio 0.14 (357kw engine, 2,558kg loaded weight); ceiling 5,500m; range 600km. Armament: 1 or 2 x Vickers 7.7mm machine gun forward, 2 x Darne 7.7mm machine gun rear; 240kg of bombs. (Artwork by Luca Canossa)

This shows Waco C-3, its original number being hidden by the green paint applied by the Paulistas. It was flown to them by a deserting pilot and became known as the '*O Waco Verde*' due to its colour. Initially an unarmed two-seater, it received a twin machine gun installed in the pilot's seat. Specifications: maximum speed 210km/h; manoeuvre ratio 0.19 (168kw engine, 920kg loaded weight); range, 868km. Armament: 2 x MG-40 7mm machine gun forward; 140kg of bombs. (Artwork by Luca Canossa)

This example, C-2, was one of three CSOs operated by the Paulistas. It was never armed properly due to the lack of suitable machine guns. Therefore, its sole protection consisted of firearms carried by the observer/co-pilot. Specifications: maximum speed 210km/h; manoeuvre ratio 0.19 (168kw engine, 920kg loaded weight); range 868km. Armament: hand-held weapons; 140kg of bombs. (Artwork by Luca Canossa)

This was the only NiD.72 operated by the Paulistas. It remains unclear if the aircraft was painted in white or silver dope overall, but – ironically – it was nicknamed '*Negrinho*' ('Little Black'). Specifications: maximum speed 260km/h; manoeuvre ratio 0.3 (447kw engine, 1,471kg loaded weight); ceiling 8,200m; range 400km. Armament: 2 x Vickers machine guns forward. (Artwork by Luca Canossa)

The Paulistas acquired a total of 10 Curtiss O-1E Falcons, and the four which eventually saw service all operated as bombers. This example, nicknamed '*Kavuré-y*', was either shot down or crashed by accident while attacking a cruiser in Santos. Specifications: maximum speed 224km/h; manoeuvre ratio 0.16 (324kw engine, 1,972kg loaded weight); ceiling 4,600m; range 1,041km. Armament: 2 x Browning machine guns forward, 2 x Browning machine guns rear; 91kg of bombs. (Artwork by Luca Canossa)

Paulista Latécoère 26 bomber. Originally a civilian transport operated by the Aeropostal Company, it was converted for combat purposes and – because the Paulistas are not known to have ever developed standardised 'national' markings – apparently continued to serve in its civilian colours. Its first bombing mission against the Federal fleet was cancelled. Specifications: maximum speed 188km/h; ceiling 4,700m; range 680km. Armament: 540kg of bombs. (Artwork by Luca Canossa)

Paulista Volunteer of the 'Legiao Negra' ('Black Legion')

Some 10,000 'coloured' soldiers sided with the Paulista cause, some of them in the Black Legion. These troops wore locally manufactured uniforms of superior quality distributed by the MMDC, which differed from those used by the Paulista FP and Federal Army. The helmet of the French Adrian design, but locally made, was copied from helmets provided by Brazilian Great War veterans (and collectors) and was still new in Brazil at the time. The tunic was replaced with a lighter shirt and the typical white handkerchief. Note the 'Chelsea' boots (still popular in southern Brazil today) and gaiters, called 'leather shins' in Brazil. The canvas belt was based on a Federal model, but lacked any inscriptions on the buckle, and was complemented by locally made suspenders and bags. His firearms included the classic .45 Colt Single Action revolver (or one of its many imitations) and an old Mauser 1908 rifle. Inset is the Paulista flag. (Artwork by Anderson Subtil)

A 'Hunter' of the 20th (Federal) Battalion de Caçadores (Hunter Battalion)

The Hunters were light infantry units and most of the troops belonging to these units were dressed as shown here. With the Brazilian Army lacking steel helmets (these were adopted only after the end of the Paulista War), it mostly used whatever was seized from the São Paulo stocks – including Adrian helmets made of cork or steel. Their visored caps used to be common a few years earlier, but were largely replaced by this cap, jokingly known as a 'cloth helmet'. The lightweight cotton tunic without pockets was usually combined with tapered pants. This soldier is shown wearing short boots, so-called 'borzequins', complemented by 'leather shins'. His backpack was combined with a blanket wrapped around it. Based on the British Mills system, the canvas webbing was of national design, with three pouches for ammunition on each side. The soldier is shown armed with the Czechoslovak-made VZ 24 carabine. Inset is the badge of the Hunter troops. (Artwork by Anderson Subtil)

Second Lieutenant of 8th BCP (Paulistas)

The São Paulo Public Force was the largest and best-equipped among all the militias of the Brazilian federal states, and possessed more troops and better firepower than most other contemporary armed forces in Latin America. During the 1920s and 1930s, its uniforms followed the patterns of the Federal Army. Correspondingly, this soldier of the 8th BCP is shown wearing a cap (instead of the 'cloth helmet'), a British-style tunic and 'Sam Brown' leather belt, and simple shoulder patches – without 'Hungarian Lace' (a very common ornament at the time). The large holster was used to carry the 7.62mm Mauser C96 pistol of German origin, a weapon that was never used by Federal troops but found a large market among state militias. Inset are the Winchester repeating rifle Mod. 1892 (a widely used weapon, despite its age), and the São Paulo State coat of arms (created in 1932 by artist Wasth Rodrigues). (Artwork by Anderson Subtil)

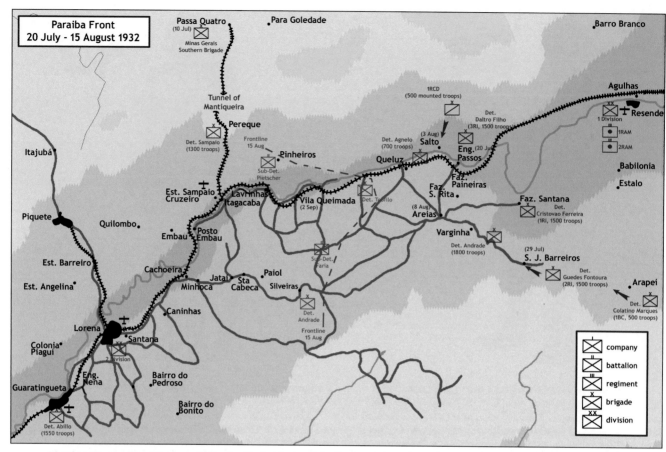

Based on Ramos, this map shows Federal units (in blue) and Paulista units (in red) as of 20 July 1932, when the Federal offensive in the Paraíba Valley began. The red line denotes Paulista positions during the second phase of the battle, when the Vila Queimada defensive line was established. Denoted in blue are dates when specific villages and other locations were taken by the Federals. The Mantiqueira Tunnel was under the control of the Paulistas at the time. (Map by Tom Cooper)

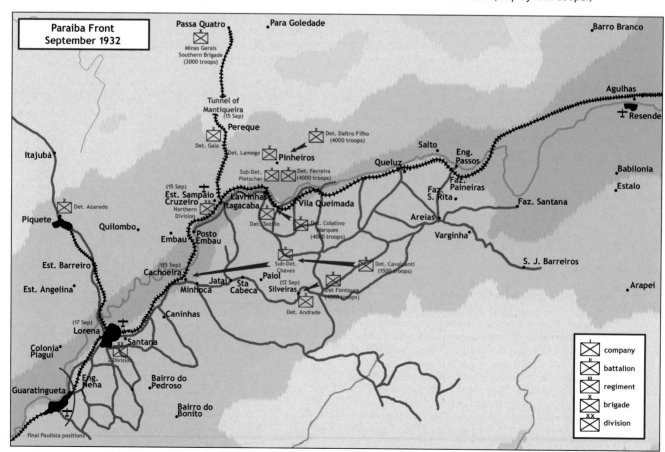

Also based on Ramos, this map shows the developments in the Paraíba Valley from 10 September 1932. Once the Federals breached the Paulista front lines, Detachment Cavalcanti rushed forward to cut off the Paulista withdrawal by taking Cachoeira, but the rebels reacted quickly and managed to retreat to Guaratinguetá. Simultaneously, the Tunnel of Mantiqueira and Piquete fronts had to be evacuated in order to prevent the troops deployed there from being cut off. (Map by Tom Cooper)

However, according to Silva, for unknown reasons and without waiting for orders, Detachment Andrade in the centre-south, retreated 29km to Silveiras, disobeying Figueiredo's orders and leaving Areias, so the counter-offensive was cancelled.[40] However, according to Ramos and Donato, Andrade only retreated when his detachment was attacked by 4th RI from Fontoura Detachment around Paredão on 8 August, being thus threatened with encirclement, although this action may not have justified such a rapid and extensive retreat.[41]

Federals scouting targets for their artillery in Queluz. Note that only the officer, armed with a pistol, has an Adrian 1915 helmet. (FGV/CPDOC/Donation by Y. Nakamura, via Donato)

10 August 1932: Fall of Queluz

With the withdrawal of Detachment Andrade, in the south, Teófilo Detachment was in a salient with its right flank in the air.[42] Once armed, all 300 soldiers of the Santos 8th BCR was sent to cover the right and the road from the abandoned Areias, now occupied by the Dictatorials. Other reinforcements arrived in the area around Morro da Fortaleza, with a company of 1st BCP sent reluctantly by Andrade, comprising only 70 soldiers from its initial 180, and still having only five of its 12 submachine guns. In the end, however, only a 14-strong combat team made it to Morro.[43] At the same time, one minor detachment under Captain Lamego was created to connect Teófilo and Andrade, operating between Queluz and Facenda São Roque.[44]

The Federal offensive resumed on 10 August, this time directly against Queluz. Detachments Daltro Filho and Ferreira attacked the Paulista '9 September' Battalion near Bianor, which to avoid being trapped was forced to retreat. The Queluz front then collapsed. Thereupon, Figueiredo ordered the construction of a new line of trenches behind, in preparation for the imminent withdrawal to Villa Queimada. He told Teófilo that he should hold for at least 24 hours, while ordering Andrade, further south, to retake Areias. Andrade, however, was unable to complete his mission. At noon, the 'Piratininga' Battalion arrived by train to reinforce Queluz, but their efforts proved too late because government forces had already taken the Morro de Fortaleza, dominating all the Paulista positions and strafing them from above and firing on the railways. The Federal envelopment of Queluz was contained on the right, but not on the left, with the defenders being partially surrounded and forced to surrender a company of 1st BCP. This also forced the right flank to retire on Queluz. Those who defended the left bank of the Paraíba were cut off by machine-gun fire from the Morro and began withdrawing en masse. The train carrying the 'Piratininga' Battalion turned back without even disembarking the troops, retiring to Villa Queimada or even Cruzeiro, where hundreds of soldiers arrived with other elements of the detachment. On the left bank, the withdrawal was made by car down the road to Pinheiros. Colonel Teófilo himself was the last to leave with his escort, sub-machine gun in hand. When the last convoy left Queluz, the bridge was blown up under enemy fire by engineer Bresser, while between 700 and 1,000 Varguistas entered the streets and fired on the fleeing trains with 4th BCP onboard, from the left flank. The disaster had

only taken a few hours to unfold, as it was still only the evening of 10 August. Apparently, Góis troops had already captured 500 Paulistas in the Paraíba Valley.[45]

10–15 August 1932: The Return of the Paulista Aviation

Back on 16 July, the UAC was withdrawn from Paraíba and concentrated on the Southern Front. This caused a government reaction that involved the establishment of a South Mixed Aviation Detachment, consisting of Federal naval aircraft and four Potezs (A-211, A-114, A-117 – which was downed – and A-115) sent successively from the Paraíba Valley.[46] This resulted in the weakening of control of the skies by the government in the valley. São Paulo took advantage of the situation to return its aviation forces and deploy them massively in Paraíba at Sermenteira airfield, Lorena, on 11–12 August.[47] Donato, however, cites preliminary actions on 10 August, so perhaps the redeployment was made over several days. He states that on this day, some Paulista aircraft were sent to bomb government formations in Salto and Areias, but mistakenly their attack fell on the rebel Andrade Detachment. Perhaps this was the reason why Andrade did not move in the planned counter-offensive to retake Areias.[48]

On 13 August, the first ever nocturnal aerial bombardment in the Western Hemisphere was flown by a Paulista Waco piloted by Captain Reynaldo Gonçalves. He took off from Lorena to bomb Resende airfield at 01:30hrs that morning. His 12 bombs all missed their target, but they certainly caused a commotion on the ground.[49] Later the same day, Potezs A-217 – flown by First Lieutenant Antonio da Silva Murici with Osvaldo Carneiro Lima as observer – and A-114 – in the hands of Captain Henrique Dyot Fontanelle with Lieutenant Marcio de Sousa e Melo – bombed the power plant in Bom Jesus de Bocaina, though without scoring any hits. It would appear that this was an attempt by Góis Monteiro to bypass the ban on Vargas carrying out any strategic bombing of São Paulo's industry: destroying the power plant would have indirectly forced a halt to be called to all rebel production. Before reaching the target, Potez A-217 ran into three Paulista aircraft: what happened afterwards is a matter of some controversy. According to one version, the rebels were bombing Federal positions around Queluz – in Alto de Laje, Fada Tatá and Capela São Roque – and at the mouth of the Mantiqueira Tunnel, and it is thus likely that they were returning from one of these sorties. However, another version says they were underway to bomb Areias, and still had no machine guns installed, so merely flew mock attacks, while Major Lysias in Potez A-116 positioned himself to attack. However, after his observer –Lieutenant Carneiro de Lima – fired only a few shots, the Federal aircraft quickly fled in the direction of Lorena.[50] On the same date, the Resende Detachment received its first fighter, a NiD.72 piloted by Lieutenant Francisco Assis Correia de Melo, an extremely able pilot known as 'Melo Maluco' and a future Minister of Brazil.[51]

Once Góis Monteiro was informed of the return of the rebel aviation, he ordered mass attacks on Lorena airfield on 14 August: one in the morning and another in the afternoon. Hagedorn states that these attacks were carried out with five Potezs and two of the newly arrived Waco Federal CSOs. Hilton agrees with the date and number of aircraft: five bombers protected by two others. However, according to Daróz the arrival of these new Wacos did not occur until 20 August, and they were not assembled and delivered for combat until the 24th, so it is unlikely that these were the new Wacos; perhaps they were the existing ones, C-4 and 'M'. Concerning the Potezs, although in theory there were 10 of them in Federal hands, no author identifies more than six by their plate numbers. As we also know that four of them were sent to the south, there could have only been two Potezs; A-216 and A-217. Of the remaining three aircraft, perhaps these were the Amiot bomber K-621 and the two NiD.72 fighters K-422 and K-423. Whatever the case, continues Hagedorn, these seven aircraft surprised all five Paulista aircraft on the ground at 09:45hrs but failed in their attack, all targets escaping unharmed. The aircraft being attacked were Potezs A-116 and A-212 and Wacos C-2, C-3, and C-5. Hilton says that a Major Ivo Borges, who was on the ground, threw his wife Celeste under a car to protect her, and tried to take off. The attack lasted only five minutes.[52] The next day, 15 August, the Paulistas attacked the Federal positions, but upon returning to Lorena they discovered that the airfield had been attacked again by government aircraft, so Lysias decided to evacuate all of the aviation to Campo de Marte, São Paulo, or perhaps even to Itapetininga in the south.[53]

10–15 August 1932: The Vila Queimada Lines

The Paraíba Valley narrowed further in the region of Vila Queimada, the river and railroad running parallel just a few meters apart. This area was cleverly chosen by Figueiredo for 2nd DIO to establish their new defensive positions after the disasters of Areias and Queluz, entrenching Detachment Teófilo here, on the right bank of the Paraíba, supported further south, by the Detachment Andrade covering the road to Silveiras. At this time Teófilo had the 'Piratininga' and 'Paes Leme' Battalions, some elements of previoussly beaten units, a company of 4th RI and some elements provided by the Sampaio Detachment, further north, that was covering the Sierra de Mantiqueira. In total, these numbered some 1,000 soldiers.

The problem was that, although well positioned, again Teófilo Ramos was in a salient, with his vanguard in Engheneiro Otalicio station, several miles east of Villa Queimada, protected by the Morros of Pedreira and Morro Verde, while his right, further forward than Detachment Andrade, in Silveiras in the south, was likely to be attacked and enveloped. To avoid this, a new small detachment was created under Captain Faria, with elements of 5th RI, which had to retreat under enemy pressure to Fazenda Tundati. To the north of Teófilo, Detachment Pinheiro was created near the Sierra de Mantiqueira. This unit was to move forward to Otalicio, but Federal resistance restricted its advance to only 5km. Therefore, Detachment Teófilo, despite the narrowness of the valley, was again in a salient, with its northern and southern sides (left and right) exposed. However, the strength of the Paulista position made the Federal advance very slow. To improve its artillery support, the government entrained a 120mm cannon from the cruiser Minas Gerais, that fired between 20 and 30 shots daily against Otalicio. In mid-August, one such projectile fell close to the trenches in Morro da Pedreira and about 150 soldiers of 4th RI and the 'Piratininga' Battalion abandoned their posts and fled to Vila Queimada. Colonel Figueiredo, who was visiting the sector, returned to his post exclaiming: 'How can you make war with people who do not fight?'[54]

Table 6: Paulista Detachments in the Paraíba Valley as of 15 August 1932		
Area	Detachment	Notes
North, vs Tunnel de Mantiqueira	Sampaio	
Centre, Vila Queimada, São Paulo railroad	Teófilo	1,000 men
Right/south: Silveiras, São Paulo road	Andrade	

On 15 or 16 August, the Morros da Pedreira and Vila do Meio, dominating Queimada and Otalicio, fell into Federal hands thanks to artillery support, despite being defended by Paulistas with automatic weapons. There only remained the Morro Verde position, which was then attacked on 16 August by 3rd Federal Battalion of 1st RI and a Pernambuco Police Company. In Morro Verde, the Paulistas had barely 100 rounds per weapon and just 50 grenades in total, so they called for reinforcements and ammunition. The rebels repulsed the first assault, but with the fall of the other two morros their position was exposed to being surrounded, so many of the soldiers fled Morro Verde. Despite this, Lieutenant Oliveira Melo and five soldiers stood their ground, and with four machine guns managed to hold back the second assault, which encouraged others to return. With some further reinforcements, it was possible to maintain the line.[55]

15–24 August: Federals Establishing Aerial Dominance

Although bad weather prevented the Federal air force from providing air support between 15 and 20 August, other kinds of sortie were flown, including some by bombers against Pedreira and Pinheiro on 16 and 19 August, and others by DH.60 Moths. Indeed, the landing gear of the aircraft crewed by Lieutenants Amarante and Murici was damaged on 19 August.[56]

On 20 August, there was the last defection of a government pilot to the Paulistas. Captain Adherbal da Costa Oliveira had faked sickness to avoid fighting the rebels, and he finally took off at the controls of one of the two fighter aircraft, Nieuport-Delage NiD.72 number K-423, from Dos Afonsos in Rio towards Resende. Arriving there, he climbed to reach the Campo de Marte in São Paulo at noon, almost out of fuel. The aircraft was later repainted, its Federal green replaced by white, yet ironically this aircraft was thereafter called 'Negrinho' ('Little Black'). Noting that the deserter's NiD continued its flight past Resende, the other loyal NiD.72, K-422 piloted by Lieutenant Murici, was sent in pursuit, but he was unable to find him in Cruzeiro, Lorena or Taubaté. Murici still tried to bomb Lorena and a convoy of animals that was heading to Cachoeira. He located two Paulista aircraft at the aerodrome at Guaratinguetá, so a massive attack against this field was prepared for the next day.[57]

On 21 August, the Federal aviation, backed up by artillery forces, managed to stop a Paulista counter-attack to regain the Morro da Pedreira.[58] On the same day, Federal Lieutenant Wanderley flew a Potez to attack a train at the Central Station, but missed his target.

The *Gazeta* revealing the defection of Captain Adherbal from the Federals to the Paulistas with his NiD.72 fighter K-423 still painted in Federal green. Although it was later painted silver, it was ironically called '*Negrinho*' ('Little Black'). (Daróz)

Meanwhile, Góis Monteiro decided to adopt a new tactic to surprise the Paulistas' small air force and destroy it on the ground. He would now always keep a group of aircraft armed and ready, which would take off only after the Paulistas were reported as flying their sorties, in order to make sure to catch them just after they landed.[59] It seems that on 21 August, an attack was launched against Guaratinguetá, and although reports are contradictory, it is possible to deduce what happened by examining the Campaign Diary of the Mixed Aviation Group and the *Gazeta*, provided by Daróz. Apparently, three Federal aircraft – Potez A-117, flown by Lieutenant Lavanére-Wanderley and Corporal Walter, Antonio Carlos da Silva Murici's Waco 'M' and NiD K-422 with Melo 'Maluco' – left Resende to attack a Paulista 'squadron' that was returning after successfully bombing an enemy concentration in Queluz. Following the new tactic of Góis Monteiro, Federal aircraft saw Guaratinguetá empty: they had arrived before the Paulistas returned! However, while turning around towards Lorena, the Federals encountered the NiD.72 K-423 and a Paulista Waco flown by Lieutenant Sylvio (probably the armed one, C-3 *Waco Verde*) at low altitude. When the rebel Waco was about to land, Sylvio saw the Federals – Wanderley's Potez and Murici's Waco – approaching the airfield at high altitude. Sylvio climbed to confront them, followed by another aircraft, and a third according to *Gazeta Paulista*, flown by Captains Adherbal and Reinaldo. The Federal Waco 'M' (Murici) spotted them and dived, strafing his opponents. He had the advantage of altitude and thus speed, both of which helped compensate for his numerical inferiority. Nevertheless, rather than flee after the 'bounce', Murici made a mistake by engaging his enemies in a classic dogfight. Sylvio managed to fire a burst from his machine gun after a looping move, but Murici avoided being hit by making a hard turn, then returned fire, as did Sylvio. Eventually, both ended up making hard horizontal turns around each other, nearly colliding in the process. Finally, Murici decided he'd had enough, diving down and fleeing, his aircraft leaving a white trail as it did so. Notably, the Federal NiD K-422 did not engage – which is why it is usually not cited in published reports of the action. This air combat was witnessed by most of the population of Lorena, which hailed and cheered the moral victory for the rebels.[60]

On 23 August, the Federals located the Paulista aircraft again and launched an attack against Guaratinguetá airfield. This time there were five attacking aircraft – two of the Potezs (A-114 and A-217), two Wacos (C-4 and 'M') and the NiD.72 K-422 – and the attack achieved great success, catching Potez A-116, Major Lysias' favourite, known as the '*Potez del Comandante*' ('Commander's Potez'), and destroying it completely.[61] It appears that almost the entire Paulista group was at the airfield, the aircraft having just returned from a ground-support mission, and they were lucky not to all be destroyed. The mission's success was in part because the Federals attacked from an unexpected direction – from the south – which meant that the rebels were caught by surprise.[62]

On 24 August, the Federals attacked the Guaratinguetá airfield

An armed Waco CTO, essentially the same as the Waco C-90s received by the government from the USA from 20 August. (Waco, via Stephen J. Hudek)

again, but only found a single aircraft there, which escaped any damage. To prevent further air strikes, the rebels evacuated all their aircraft to Campo de Marte, São Paulo and Mogi Mirim, focusing on the fight on the new Mineiro front.[63] According to Hagedorn, in the evacuation process the four rebel aircraft encountered three Federal Wacos, which attacked them without causing any damage.[64] Thereby, the loyalists had managed once again to secure control of the sky in the Paraíba Valley.

The first batch of new Waco C-90s, with plates C-7 to C-11, arrived fresh from the United States on 20 August and were assembled on the 24th. Four of them became part of Resende Detachment the following day, one of them piloted by Lieutenant Nero Moura.[65] They were subsequently sent to other fronts: two to the south on 1 September, and the three others to Minas, between 28 and 30 August. In any case, with the local aircraft already present, some six airframes (Potezs A-216 and 217, Wacos C-4 and 'M', NiD K-422 and Amiot K-621), the Federal numbers were now enough to control the valley.[66]

Table 7: Federal Combat Aircraft in the Paraíba Valley, 28–30 August 1932

Type	Plate	Main role
Potez	A-216	Bomber
Potez	A-217	Bomber
Waco	C-4	Fighter-Bomber
Waco	M	Fighter-Bomber
NiD	K-422	Fighter
Amiot	K-621	Bomber

24 August – 2 September: Breaking the Vila Queimada Line

Despite being deprived of air support, on 24 and 25 August the Paulistas organised two separate counter-attacks to recover the Morro da Pedreira.[67] Fortunately for them, bad weather also prevented Varguista air actions until 29 August.[68] Although the 'Piratininga' Battalion, supported by two assault companies from Major Agnelo failed in the offensive, a third attack made by civilians from the Southern Front under Saldanha da Gama achieved progress on the flanks thanks to artillery support from 2nd GIAP and entered the Federal trenches. With Morro da Pedreira retaken, this company was elevated to the rank of 'Saldanha' Battalion.[69] Yet it was upgraded only by name, with the number of soldiers remaining that of a mere company at about 100.

However, the problem of lack of ammunition began to be added to the occasional lack of fighting spirit for the first time. The Paulista factories only made projectiles for Krupp guns, so that once depleted, the Schneider guns had to be retired and evacuated to Lavrinhas. In the meantime, the northern flank of Detachment Faria was cleared by the Federals, its troops retiring under pressure to the heights west of Fundati on 1 September.[70] The loyalists now began once again to attack Morro Verde, where the Paulistas had a mere 10 cartridges per soldier. After three days of attacks, the rebels received so little ammunition that it ran out after just 10 minutes' fighting. Figueiredo, realising the flanks of the position would fall, ordered the construction of a new line of trenches behind, in Lavrinhas, in preparation for a new retreat.[71]

On 29 August, there were occasional attacks by Federal Wacos, one piloted by Lieutenant Nero Moura, on the new Lavrinhas lines in the rebel rear. These attacks probably included the new Wacos as they returned from Pouso Alegre to Resende that day, before definitively flying back to Minas again the next day.[72] On 30 August, the attacks against 'Paes de Leme' Battalion (later named 'Fernão Sales') under Major Pietscher (Detachment Pietscher) became unbearable.[73] The Federals slowly made a trench approach that came to within a few metres of the rebels, firing at them from 07:00hrs until 17:00hrs. Firing resumed on 1 September at 08:00hrs, accompanied by an artillery bombardment until 11:00hrs. Although Daróz says that the Federal Aviation did not appear due to bad weather, the truth is that on that day Lieutenants Lampert and Fontenelle released three bombs on a locomotive between Lavrinhas and Vila Queimada, and then they made three passes on a truck convoy. In a second attack, Lampert dropped 12 bombs against the same convoy. Also at this time, another Federal Potez bombed a paddock of 50 animals in Cruzeiro, but fortunately for them, none were harmed.[74]

After the bombing, the Federals screamed out of their trenches, rushed forward and engaged in hand-to-hand fighting with the bayonet, taking the two lines of Paulista trenches once the rebels had exhausted their ammunition. Lieutenant Washington Oliveira had to cover their retreat by throwing three grenades, allowing them to withdraw about 400 metres after crossing the river, while Federal machine guns were placed in the newly taken positions. With the right flank crumbling, at the suggestion of 2nd GIAP's Captain Arcy, who warned that they were going to be enveloped, Figueiredo ordered the withdrawal of Teófilo Detachment to Lavrinhas on the night of 2 September.[75] The Pietscher Detachment was positioned on the height north-west of Vila Queimada.[76] Thus, after 18 days of fighting, the Vila Queimada lines fell into the hands of the Varguistas. The only reaction was a Paulista counter-attack in Silveiras, at the southern (right) end of the line on 3 September, which managed to snatch some positions back from 19th BC, that was threatening the city, but eventually they had to retire again.[77]

Reporter Armando Brussolo, on the left of the locomotive, going to Piquete.
(Museu da Imagem e don Som de São Paulo, via Donato)

Covering the North Flank: The Sierra de Mantiqueira

While all this fighting had taken place in the eastern part of the Paraíba Valley, involving the central Paulista detachments, we must go back to mid-July to see what was happening on the northern (or left) flank of the rebels. There, as we have said, Detachment Sampaio was watching the Sierra de Mantiqueira, some 1,800 metres high, the north–south accesses that linked the state of Minas Gerais with the rebels in the Paraíba Valley. This route, once forced by the government, would cut the communications of the Paulista 2nd DIO and encircle all the rebel units. The detachment was formed on 20 July by half of 1st Battalion (two or three companies) and all of 2nd Battalion of 5th RI, along with two companies of 5th BCP, a total of up to 1,300 soldiers.[78]

Further to the rear, guarding the ammunition factory in Piquete, and the railway route that connected with Minas Gerais, was Detachment Abilio, which on 17 July had 4th Cavalry Squadron of 4th RCD (a fragment of the Federal 4th Division went over to the rebels) and 3rd (less one company) and 2nd Battalions of 6th RI. These were all located in Piquete itself, numbering some 1,000 soldiers in total. A little further south, in Barreira station, was 1st BCPR, with about 500 men, and further south, in Lorena, the stocks and logistics units of 6th RI. Fortunately for the Paulistas this sector was not attacked by the Federals, so it acted as a kind of general reserve for the Paraíba, and these troops would later be sent to the Minas front.[79]

On the Federal side, in Minas Gerais, across the range of the Sierra de Mantiqueira, there were initially elements of 4th Infantry Division. Some fragments of 11th RI under Major Herculano Assumpção came from São João de Rei, while 4th RCD and 10th RI came from Tres Coraçoes under Alexandre Zacarias in Assumpção, which also contained the Paulista's 5th RI. A patrol from the latter unit under Lieutenant Melchiades Tavares da Silva moved from Lorena to take Passa Quatro in Minas on 10 July, destroying railroad bridges, until they were expelled by a counter-attack. On 14 July, the first three brigades of Minas State troops were formed, of which the Southern Brigade under Colonel Lery occupied the Túnel de Mantiqueira front, with its headquarters in Lavras, defending Passa Quatro, Manacá and the Mantiqueira tunnel, just 30–34km from the Paulista Cruzeiro base. Cruzeiro was an important transportation link as all reinforcements and supplies had to pass through Cruzeiro to be moved to the eastern end of the valley. Four days later, the regular troops of 4th RCD and the 2nd Battalion of 11th RI, 4th Division, which were

Paulista soldiers in Cruzeiro, the main supply base and vital communications link for the Paraíba Valley. Note the Mk I helmet of the trooper. (Museu da Imagem e do Som de São Paulo, via Donato)

Women from Lorena giving food to Paulista soldiers of 2nd Battalion Liga da Liga de Defesa Paulista. Note the Adrian M1915 helmets. (Museu da Imagem e do Som de São Paulo; via Donato)

Officer Doctor Juscelino Kubitschek, a future president of Brazil, serving in the Mantiqueira sector. (FGV/ CPDOC/ Arquivo Gustavo Capanema, via Donato)

Morro do Cristal, Garupa and Sierra de Itaguaré; and the left in Fazenda Gomeira. Over the following weeks these troops were reinforced and eventually included 3,289 soldiers (with 2,505 rifles, 20 machine guns and 125 sub-machine guns). They comprised the 1st (with 794 men), 2nd (445), 3rd (394), 7th (741) and 8th (422) Battalions of FP Mineiros, the 19th Provisional, or *Provisorio*, Battalion (324) and the Mineira Cavalry (232), all supported by six artillery pieces of the 10th RAM, two from the 8th RAM and a three-tank section. However, these theoretical figures were greatly reduced due to the large number of casualties caused by the harsh winter conditions in the high mountains. In fact, between 17 July and 31 August an incredible 1,016 soldiers were hospitalised, 214 of them from wounds and the others as a result of disease. Among the physicians who served in this sector was Juscelino Kubitschek, a future president of Brazil.[81]

Table 8: Ground Units on the Tunnel de Mantiqueira Front, July–August 1932		
Federalists		
Initial forces, departing mid-July	**Departing**	**Notes**
4th RCD	18 July	
II/11th RI	18 July	
One battalion/10th RI	Later	
Artillery Section/8th RAM	Stayed	2 pieces
Tank Section	Stayed	3 Renault-17 tanks
Forces in mid-August		
Southern Minas Gerais Brigade (Colonel Lery)		
1st FPM Battalion		794 soldiers
2nd FPM Battalion		445 soldiers
3rd FPM Battalion		394 soldiers
7th FPM Battalion		741 soldiers
8th FPM Battalion		422 soldiers
Provisorio (Provisional) 19th Battalion		324 soldiers
Mineiro Cavalry		232 riders
10th RAM		6 artillery pieces
8th RAM		2 artillery pieces
Assault Tank Section		3 Renault-17s

guarding the tunnel, were replaced by local Mineiras troops. Those regular troops then reinforced the Mineiro front, in the north-west. The only regular units to stay in this area were a battery of the 10th RI (which later would also depart), two sections of the 8th RAM of Pouso Alegre and a Tank Assault Section, consisting of three Renault 17 tanks, one with a 37mm gun and two with machine guns.[80] These units had their headquarters in Manacá, which controlled access to Morro de Cristal, and thence to the Sierra de Itaguaré and the mouth of the tunnel. These formed, together with Minas Gerais troops, three sub-sectors: the tunnel in the centre; the right in Fazenda São Benito,

Table 8: Ground Units on the Tunnel de Mantiqueira Front, July–August 1932

Total		3,289 soldiers (2,505 rifles, 20 machine guns, 125 sub-machine guns, 8 artillery pieces and 3 tanks).
Paulistas (20 July)		
Detachment Sampaio (future Northern Division)		
2-3 Companies, 1st Battalion/5th RI	Some 200–300 men	
2nd Battalion/5th RI	Some 500 men	
3rd Battalion/5th RI	Some 500 men	
2 Companies, 5th BCP	Some 200 men	
3 Companies, 2nd BCP	Some 300 men	
1 battery, 2nd GIAP	Some 100 men	
1 battery, 2nd GAD	Some 100 men	
Total:	2,000 soldiers (8 artillery pieces)	

14–21 July 1932: Paulista Resistance in the Tunnel

The most stubborn struggle was in the Mantiqueira tunnel itself. There, Paulistas seized the tunnel on 13 July with 2nd BCP and two infantry companies and one machine-gun company of 5th RI. In the Perequé sector, on the railroad track behind the tunnel, some elements of 2nd Battalion of 5th RI guarding the area were instructed not to fire on any troops coming from Minas as they doubted whether the state would ally with the Paulistas. This permitted the Federal 4th RCD, from Tres Coraçoes in Minas, under the aggressive Colonel Eurico Gaspar Dutra, to reach the mouth of the tunnel on 16 July.[82]

There was harsh fighting between 14 and 18 July. Troops of 2nd Battalion, 5th RI panicked on the 15th, fleeing from the front, so it was necessary to replace this unit with the 3rd and 4th Caçadores Companies.[83] On the 18th, the government seemed about to take the tunnel, but fortunately for the rebels 2nd BCP and the 3rd Battalion of 5th RI arrived under Major Gaia and the situation stabilised on the 19th, remaining so until near the end of the conflict in mid-September.[84]

However, clashes continued until then at other points around the tunnel. The most advanced and highest Paulista points, the peaks of Gomeira, Crystal, Itaguaré and Gomeirinha which dominated the rail route over Cruzeiro, were attacked by Minas government troops from the Southern Brigade, right subsector, on 10, 16 and 22 July.

On the 27th, with the sector almost enveloped, the line of the four peaks was eventually abandoned. The Federals had attacked here with two army units and 1,500 Mineiros. However, the rebels retreated only a short way behind their lines and remained in the tunnel itself.[85] The positions had been reinforced by a company located in Entre Rios on the left side, and two companies and a machine-gun section taken from Areias in the south-central sector, from Andrade Detachment, on the 21st.[86] On 30 July, the Paulistas counter-attacked with artillery and machine-gun fire in these sectors, killing Lieutenant Colonel Fulgencio de Sousa Santos.[87]

4–19 August: Resistance In Batedor

The Paulista left flank was set at Batedor, where it passed a road from Minas that linked with Guaratinguetá, in the rear of São Paulo, parallel to the rail line situated further east in the Mantiquiera tunnel. On 22 July, a recruit company under Captain Azeredo was sent there, and was gradually increased by successive reinforcements up to some 800 soldiers along with a 75mm artillery piece. There was no action in the Batedor sector until 4 August, when the first government patrols appeared resulting in a clash that ended at close quarters, using bayonets and grenades, but the attackers were unable to take the position.[88] The Federal attacks continued on the left subsector/ Southern Brigade on 9 August, this time on the other end of the line, in Capela São Roque, forcing the rebels to retire to Pinheiros the next day in order to avoid being cut off once they had exhausted their ammunition. On 11 August, on the left side of the line, when it seemed that the Paulistas had achieved at least the neutrality of Minas Gerais, 600 men of the 3rd Mineiro FP Battalion attacked the outpost of Barreira, defended by just 80 soldiers of the 5th BCP, who managed to retreat intact cross-country but the position fell.[89] Some help came from the Paulista aviation, which on 13 August bombed Federal positions in the Alto do Laje, Fada Tatá, Capela São Roque and the mouth of the tunnel.[90]

The Paulista side of the Tunnel de Mantiqueira, with a wagon car blocking the railroad. (PGV/CPDOC, Arquivo Gustavo Capanema, Careta 1/10/1932, via Donato)

Paulistas armed with machine guns entrenched in the Tunnel de Mantiqueira. (Waldemar Martins Ferreira Filho, via Donato)

Thereafter, the Federal attacks continued.[91] An assault by three companies took place on 17 August, with artillery and heavy machine guns in support, taking Batedor before being expelled by a counter-attack. The struggle continued until 19 August, when government *vermelinhos* (the Waco aircraft painted red) strafed rebel positions.[92] However, the Paulistas remained in their positions, despite additional attacks such as the one of 4 September, in which Figueiredo, visiting the front, had to distribute hand grenades to his escort for self-defence.[93] The Paulistas only yielded in mid-September with the fall of the entire southern flank, which forced the whole sector to retreat without having been beaten.

Overall Situation in September 1932

As of 10 September, the general situation across the front of the Paraíba Valley was that the rebel front line ran first from west to east, parallel to the boundary of the Sierra de Mantiqueira to Batedor and the tunnel (the far left, in the north), and then turned to the right (or south) to Fazenda Boa Vista, Pinheiros and Lavrinhas, until it reached Silveiras. The rebel deployment began in the area of the Sierra, with the so-called Northern Division, under Colonel Sampaio, which was formed by the Batedor Detachment of Lieutenant Colonel Azeredo and the Túnel Detachment of Lieutenant Colonel Gaia, which, as we have just seen, had successfully defended its position throughout the war, and even managed to lend a company of 2nd BCP to the next detachment located further to the south.[94]

In the central sector of the valley, Detachment Pinheiros was the weakest on the whole front, with few soldiers and the first unit looking directly to the east without the protection of the Mantequeira range (where the bulk of Federal troops were placed), under Lieutenant Colonel Lamego, later replaced by Lieutenant Colonel Veloso. Located from the foothills of the Sierra and into the valley, it was poorly connected to the following Paulista detachments, and its area of Fazenda Boa Vista, to the north, was under heavy pressure from the Varguistas; its fall would threaten the encircling of the Batedor and Túnel Detachments. Further south was the small detachment of Major Pietscher, formed only of the '*Paes Leme*' Battalion and FP elements of Captain Valenca, that served as liaison with the next main detachment. That force was led by Lieutenant Colonel Teófilo Ramos, with his command post in Lavrinhas, covering the São Paulo–Rio railway, which now had a heavy 150mm cannon mounted on a railway platform to counteract the 120mm guns of the Federals.[95]

Finally, at the far right, or south, of the line and looking to the south-east, was the small detachment of Major Chaves. Under heavy enemy pressure, it served as liaison to the other major detachment of the valley, that of Colonel Andrade on the São Paulo–Rio road, with its headquarters in Silveiras.[96] In the rear and looking towards the coast was Detachment Veiga-Abreu, controlling the Cunha sector against the loyalist troops that had landed on the coast. All supplies for this force passed through the city of Cruzeiro upon which they were dependent.[97]

An analysis of rebel units shows that in mid-September they had only about 8,000 combatants on this front in contradiction to the oft quoted 20,000. Thus, it is highly unlikely that they could suddenly boast some 10,000–12,000 more a week before this attack. As almost always in this war, the government troops enjoyed a numerical superiority of at least two to one.[98]

Regarding the Federals, the four main detachments of the Army Detachment of the East ran from north to south, the first being that of Daltro Filho (against the rebel positions at Pinheiros), then came Ferreira, that of Colatino Marques and finally the Fontoura Detachment, at the southern end, opposite Silveiras on the railroad. To these was added a fifth detachment created on 9 September under Newton Cavalcanti. According to Góis Monteiro's plan, Detachment Cavalcanti remained in reserve, consisting of the Bahia FP, Goiás and Piaui Battalions, with the mission to occupy the region of Cachoeira. To do this, the Fontoura Detachment would break the front and then Cavalcanti would go through the gap up to Cachoeira Paulista, the rear point where the railway and the main road from São Paulo to Rio converged. Such a move would cut off all the Paulista forces. Góis ordered Cavalcanti's troops to be specially trained in the tactics of mobile warfare by 100 drill sergeants for two weeks, to move at maximum speed regardless of their flanks in a kind of 'Brazilian Blitzkrieg'.[99]

As for the number of government troops involved, on 1 October, 10 Federal detachments of the Eastern Detachment Army (both in Minas and the Paraíba) had between 34,000 and 40,000 combatants (approximately 3,500–4,000 per detachment).[100] Five of these detachments were in Minas, and the other five in Paraíba.[101] We may deduce that there were some 21-22,000 men in the Paraíba around 10 September from these and other data (see Table 11). Once again, the Federals thus possessed twice the number of combatants in comparison to the Paulistas.

Table 9: Detachments in the Paraíba Valley, September 1932

Paulistas		
Northern Division	**Col. Sampaio (Túnel/Batedor)**	
Detachments	**Location**	
Azeredo	Batedor	
Gaia	Mantiqueira Tunnel	
2nd DIO	Col. Figueiredo (Paraíba Valley)	
Detachments	Location	Notes
Lamego (then Veloso)	Pinheiro	
Pietscher		Minor link detachment
Teófilo Ramos	Lavrinhas (Rio railway)	150mm railway gun
Chaves		Minor link detachment
Andrade	Silveiras (Rio road)	
Veiga Abreu	Cunha (Coast)	
Total: 10,000–12,000 men		
Federals		
Eastern Army Detachment (Gen. Góis Monteiro)		
(Excluding 4th Division units fighting in the Minas Gerais front)		
Detachments	**Location**	**Notes**
Southern Minas Brigada (Lery)	Tunnel-Batedor	3,000 soldiers (only until Sept 13)
Daltro Filho	Vs Pinheiros	4,000–4,500 soldiers
Ferreira		4,000–4,500 soldiers
Colatino Marques		4,000–4,500 soldiers
Fontoura	Vs Silveiras	4,000–4,500 soldiers
Newton Cavalcanti	Reserve (to attack Cachoeira)	1,500 soldiers
Total: 21,000–22,000 men		

4–16 September 1932: Reinforcements for the Federalists

As mentioned previously, three new Federalists Wacos had been redeployed to the Minas sector on 30 August. By 4 September there were five Wacos (serials C-12 to C-16) in the Paraíba sector at Dos Afonsos airfield, four days later, three of them had joined the Resende Detachment and promptly flew close air-support sorties.[102]

Lieutenant Lampert flew bombing and strafing missions against a rebel column, a truck convoy and a railway bridge near Silveiras on 4 September. The same day, a reconnaissance flight detected preparations for a new rebel retreat to Silveiras, in turn prompting Góis to accelerate preparations to launch a new offensive. On 5 September, Lampert bombed a column that was heading for Lorena and consequently fled to Cachoeira, while Melo 'Maluco' bombed a number of trucks in Silveiras. The flames of the burning trucks reached the Paulista trenches.[103]

On 10 September, the freighter SS *Northern Prince* arrived with the third batch of five Wacos, that were quickly assembled and incorporated into the Mixed Aviation Group on 13 September, receiving the consecutive registrations C-17 to C-21.[104] Three days later, aircraft with the registrations C-18, C-20 and C-21 – all meanwhile equipped with radios and reconnaissance cameras – were sent to the Resende Detachment.[105]

With this, there were 10 new Wacos in the Paraíba Valley by 21 September (with six others in the south), registered as C-12 to C-21.

To these, the Federalists could add the old C-4 and 'M', two Potezs (A-216 and A-217), one NiD.72 (K-422) and one Amiot (K-621), for a theoretical total of 16 aircraft. Periodically, these were further reinforced by up to 11 other aircraft (including five combat aircraft) from the Littoral Air Force.[106]

The Paulistas seem to have been quick to react to these moves. At an unspecified date – probably on 13 September, and certainly before the fall of Lorena four days later – two Wacos and two Potezs (probably including the A-212, alias 'Nosso Potez'/'Our Potez') were dispatched from the Mineiro front to the Paraíba Valley. After stopping in Lorena, they bombed Federalist trenches, convoys and the railway in Queluz. There are also reports of five other Paulista aircraft attacking loyalist units operating in the coastal area of Cunha.[107] Such reports are dubious, because the Paulistas are known to have been down to only two Potezs, of which one (A-116) had been destroyed on 23 August. Thus, it is technically impossible for two of them to have flown combat operations in September. More likely, the Paulistas did react, but with fewer aircraft than usually cited.

On 13 September, in preparation for the Federal offensive, Góis Monteiro ordered the bombing of Lorena by what was sometimes called the 'Bomber Platoon'. This unit – the precise composition of which is not recorded – was escorted by the 'Fighter Platoon' with its one NiD (K-422) flown by Lieutenant Melo 'Maluco' and a military Waco flown by Lieutenant Jose Sampaio Macedo. From what can be concluded on the basis of diverse reports, the Federalist fighters intercepted and pursued a Paulista formation as it fled in the direction of Lorena, but without success.[108]

Table 10: Combat Aircraft in the Paraíba Valley, September 1932

Main Base: Resende			
Type	**Plate**	**Role**	**Notes**
Waco	C-12	Fighter-Bomber	
Waco	C-13	Fighter-Bomber	
Waco	C-14	Fighter-Bomber	
Waco	C-15	Fighter-Bomber	
Waco	C-16	Fighter-Bomber	
Waco	C-17	Fighter-Bomber	

Waco	C-18	Recce	Radio & camera
Waco	C-19	Fighter-Bomber	
Waco	C-20	Recce	Radio & camera
Waco	C-21	Recce	Radio & camera
Waco	C-4	Fighter-Bomber	
Waco	'M'	Fighter	Used for escort missions with its synchronised machine guns
Potez	A-216	Bomber	
Potez	A-217	Bomber	
NiD.72	K-422	Fighter	
Amiot	K-621	Bomber	In Dos Afonsos, Rio

9–12 September: Federal Offensive in Silveiras-Pinheiros

The situation for the Paulistas was becoming desperate. A general lack of ammunition and weapons produced a collapse in morale, which was increased by the successive withdrawals, and Figueiredo had to start placing guards and controls on roads and railways to arrest deserters. Foreseeing a new collapse, Figueiredo had already ordered the preparation of a line of trenches to the rear, in Engheneiro Neiva, east of Guaratinguetá, and tried to convince the Paulista supreme commander, General Klinger, to make such a withdrawal before being attacked. He also wanted to reduce the front line by evacuating the Mantiquiera tunnel and Batedor posts, and save troops that could be sent to defend Campinas, on the Minas front, as he considered

Engheneiro Neiva Station, one of the last defensive lines of the Paulistas on the Paraíba Valley front. (Museu do Telefone, via Donato)

correctly that the loss of this would be more disastrous than Cruzeiro. However, according to Klinger, the evacuation of Cruzeiro would definitively lower rebel morale, and before any decision could be made, the long-awaited major government offensive began on 11 September.[109]

Since 9 September, the Federal Fontoura Detachment had occupied the first defensive positions of Silveiras after the flight of the Paulista 4th RI, at the southern (or right) end of the line, where the Paulista Detachment Andrade was located along the São Paulo–Rio road.[110] On 11 September, the loyalists moved directly against Silveiras itself, and as the attack continued all night, all ammunition reserves from 2nd DIO were sent to Andrade.[111] However, to the surprise of the rebels, in a perfectly coordinated action by Góis Monteiro, the Pinheiros sector, on the right (north) end of the line was also attacked by Detachment Daltro Filho on the morning of 12 September.[112] This attack fell on the meagre forces of Veloso, the weakest point of the rebel deployment. When the ammunition reserves were exhausted, they were only restocked by taking supplies from sectors not under attack at Batedor, Mantiquiera Tunnel and Lavrinhas, but this merely shifting the shortages around. By 13:00hrs, Veloso's troops had exhausted their ammunition and abandoned their positions, but Donato says that this only was only done at 17:00hrs, by which time they had only 30 remaining rounds in total.[113] Federal forces then occupied Fazenda Boa Vista, from which they could direct artillery fire against Lavrinhas and Cruzeiro itself in the heart of the rebel deployment, in addition to cutting off the retreat of the Batedor and Mantiqueira Tunnel Detachments. Thereupon, Figueiredo ordered the withdrawal of the whole front to Cruzeiro at 16:00hrs.[114] With the retirement of the Paulistas from Mantiqueira, on 13 September Colonel Lery Mineira's Brigade was sent to reinforce Brigade Amaral, already in Minas.[115] On the previous day, the Federal Detachment Guedes Fontoura had managed to take Silveiras, at the southern end of the line, from Andrade, opening another hole in the rebel positions.[116] During the offensive, Góis issued orders on 8, 10, and 11–13 September emphasising air support.[117]

13–16 September: Great Withdrawal to Guaratinguetá

On 13 September, the Paulista Detachment Veloso was on the heights east of Córrego Jacu, the Pietscher Detachment retreated in the direction of Colegio, that of Teófilo began its withdrawal from eastern Lavrinhas, Andrade left Silveiras for the Santa Cabeça–Jataí line and Saldanha remained in Cachoeira and Ponte de Embaú. From there, all forces began a general withdrawal to the region of Guaratinguetá. Covering the retreat was a rearguard force in the line Santa Cabeça–Jataí–Cachoeira–Ponta de Embaú, in a semicircle south-east of Cruzeiro, comprising Detachment Gaia (two BCP battalions, the 'Otaviano' and 'Inojosa', located north-east of the railroad in Embaú) and Andrade Detachment (formed by elements of 2nd RCD, 4th BCR and 'Azaredo' Battalion, covering Jataí, south-east of the railroad, along the Rio–São Paulo highway).[118] That same day, the three government Wacos from Resende Detachment bombed Silveiras, Pinheiro and Lavrinhas, increasing the chaos among the rebels shortly before the arrival of the Varguistas.[119]

On 14 September, Cavalcanti Detachment, maintained as the Federal reserve, took advantage of the gap produced by Guedes taking Silveiras to rapidly advance on Cachoeira Paulista, which it occupied that day.[120] This cut communications between São Paulo and the Cruzeiro, Mantiquiera and Silveiras areas, which threatened the destruction of 2nd DIO and all the rebel troops in the Paraíba Valley. The railway between Cachoeira and Lavrinhas created an arc, with the curve facing outward, so that the path of retreat was greater than

A Federal Waco *vermelinho*, strangely without any plate marker on the tail, and a DH-60 Moth behind, at the Resende air base. (Daróz)

Cachoeira bridge, destroyed by the Paulistas when retiring in September. (Museu do Telefone, São Paulo, via Donato)

a train packed with fugitives only stopped at Taubaté, where they had to be disarmed and held by the '*Paranhos*' Battalion. The Guaratinguetá withdrawal, over some 50km, was the largest of the war.[124] However, although the Paulistas, with the evacuation of Sampaio's Northern Division in Mantiquiera, saved troops and reduced their front line, the Federals were also able to remove the 3,289 soldiers located there to reinforce the Mineiro front.[125]

17 September: Fall of Lorena

By 16 September, the front had stabilised and the Paulista 2nd DIO could finally settle into their defensive positions in eastern Guaratinguetá in a line from west of Colonia Piagui to Engheneiro Neiva Station and the Quebra Cangalhas ridges to the south-east.[126] In the meantime, Detachment Gaia continued to delay progress by the Federal forces, being formed of two companies of the '*Saldanha Gama*' Battalion that were expelled from Canas when their ammunition ran out on 17 September after an assault by two government battalions and

the straight route made from Silveiras by Cavalcanti. Fortunately for the Paulistas, a rapid withdrawal was made by Figueiredo, who was able to save all his troops, covered by the rearguard detachment. In the meantime, airstrikes from the Resende Air Detachment continued bombing Cachoeira, facilitating the entry of Cavalcanti into the city.[121] On the 15th, the Paulista Gaia Detachment continued its retreat to the south-west to take up positions in Canas, covering the retreat of the rebel main force on the railroad east of Guaratinguetá.[122] Meanwhile, a solitary government aircraft bombed Jundiaí from high altitude, but without appreciable results.[123]

Figueiredo's retreat, despite being a defeat, was a major logistical success, evacuating all detachments, including civilians, in Cruzeiro and their heavy machinery in just one night. The most difficult part of the operation to accept was the eviction of the detachments in Batedor and the Mantiqueira Tunnel at the northern end of the line, despite them not being defeated and indeed containing the enemy for nearly two months. Nevertheless, the rush to escape and the defeat took their toll on the troops, with units starting to dissolve during the retreat. For example, on 13 September, some trains full of evacuated troops did not stop when they arrived at Pinda station but tried to go directly to São Paulo, considering that the war was over for them. In the Mantiquiera Tunnel, on 14 September, some 16 deserters from 2nd FP Battalion and 4th and 5th RI were jailed. In the same area, on the 15th,

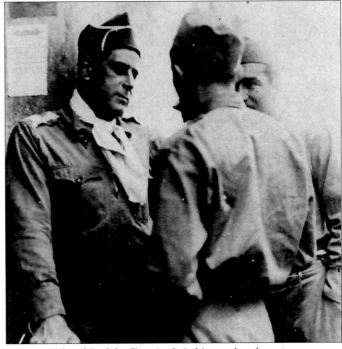

Colonel Euclides Figueiredo in his new headquarters in Aparecida do Norte in mid-September 1932. Note his typical headquarters cap and the long white handkerchief. During this time he directed the masterful Guaratinguetá withdrawal. (Waldemar Martins Ferreira Filho, via Donato)

Lorena factories bombed by the Federals before being captured on 19 September. (Museo do Telefone, São Paulo, via Donato)

The armoured train 'Fantasma da Morte', in action in the Mogiana region. Note the camouflage pattern. (Coleção Paulo Florençano, Taubaté, via Donato)

The Federal headquarters in Cruzeiro in mid-September 1932. Note the Mk I and Adrian helmets of the officers. (FGV/CPDOC/ Donation from Y. Nakamura, via Donato)

72 hours of artillery preparation.[127] This unit's FPP Cavalry Regiment received 343 shell strikes from 105mm, 120mm and 155mm guns within an area of just 300 metres. The rebel artillery responded with only 20 75mm shells and a few from 120mm guns.[128] Nevertheless, the retreat was made in perfect order, and they were in Lorena by the afternoon, which was also evacuated under Figueiredo's orders, along with its civilians. The Paulista Number 6 Armoured Train, known as 'Fantasma da Morte' ('Death Phantom'), equipped with machine guns and a Krupp 75mm cannon, along with a motorised truck equipped with machine guns, helped contain the Varguistas that were hard on their heels. The train ran over several pro-government civilians in Lorena who tried to break the tracks and derail it. Eventually, the 'Saldanha' Battalion continued to cover the withdrawal.[129] On top of the loss of Lorena, the Paulistas suffered another serious blow with the fall of Piquete, further north, where the main Paulista ammunition factory was located, and another railroad that linked with Minas. Finally, on the Coast Front, the Cunha Detachment, facing the sea, was also forced to retire from 16–18 September to avoid being isolated from the rightmost Paraíba detachment.

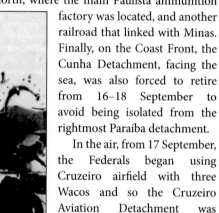

In the air, from 17 September, the Federals began using Cruzeiro airfield with three Wacos and so the Cruzeiro Aviation Detachment was created.[130] As Lorena fell into government hands, the Federals also began to use the airfields of the city from 20 September.[131]

On 18 September, the desperate rebels sent Potez A-212, known as 'Nosso Potez' and the only one still operational for the Paulistas, under Major Lysias and Machado Bittencourt on a propaganda mission throwing pamphlets over government lines.[132] With total air dominance by the Federals, they were soon intercepted over Cruzeiro by a patrol consisting of two Wacos and a Potez, who dived down and fired on them. With ammunition exhausted or their machine guns having jammed, Lysias resorted to making close passes, feinting to hit his opponents. The Federals, seeing the actions of this 'crazy' major and the absurdity of the situation, decided to break off the encounter.[133] Lysias survived the clash, although when he returned to base his aircraft had more than 50 bullet holes.[134]

18 September: Showdown in Guará

Meanwhile, the Paulistas were reorganised into new detachments to defend the new front line of Guará or Guaratinguetá. As a vanguard, in the north-east, was a small contingent under Captain Armando Figueiredo north of Lorena. Behind them in the north (or left flank) was Lieutenant Colonel Gaia's subsector, from Pigüaí to the Paraíba River, with 2nd RCD, 5th RI, the 'Legião Negra' ('Black Legion') Battalion, Captain Sandy's Company, the 'Bento Gonçalves' Battalion, the Bombarda Company and 5th BCPR, in all about 3,300 soldiers. Further south, in the centre, was Lieutenant Colonel Rodrigues Telemaco's subsector, along the Paraíba River and the railroad, formed by the Herbert and Fournier companies and elements of 4th RI, with perhaps some 700 men. Along the Rio–São Paulo highway on the extreme right was Colonel Sampaio's subsector, with the Espindola, Paes Leme and Azeredo Battalions, and Boaventura, Braz Nogueira (or Texeira), and Jacques Felix companies and the Valença

A Paulista Potez being prepared for a mission. Note the Paulista white band painted on the fuselage, the machine-gun seat of the co-pilot and the Adrian 1915 helmet of the crew member on the left. (Della Rosa, via Historia y Vida)

Squadron, comprising a total of about 1,300 men. As a reserve, under Colonel Andrade in the Maia-Marcondes region, north-west of Guara, to reinforce the Gaia Detachment if necessary, were the remnants of the former Detachment Andrade, made up of 6th RI, a *Bombardas* Company and a company of 12th RI (one of the few Mineiros units that joined the Paulistas), perhaps an additional 2,200 soldiers. Finally, in Matadouro Guara, on the right bank of the Paraíba and to reinforce Sampaio if necessary, there were some 600 soldiers of Lieutenant Colonel Teófilo Ramos, with the *Otaviano* and *Inojosa* Battalions.[135] In total, all these forces comprised some 8,100 Paulista soldiers to cover a

Table 11: Detachments on the Guaratinguetá Front

Front Line in Guaratinguetá (18 Sept)

Paulistas

Detachments	Location	Composition
Captain Figueiredo	Vanguard, north Lorena	
Gaia	Left flank: Piguaí to Paraíba	2nd RCD, 5th RI, 'Legião Negra' Battalion, Captain Sandy's Company, 'Bento Gonçalves' Battalion, Bombarda Company, 5th BCP
Rodrigues Telemaco	Centre: Paraíba River/railroad	Herbert & Fournier Companies, elements of 4th RI
Sampaio	Right: Rio–São Paulo highway	Battalions Espindola, Paes Leme, Azeredo. Companies Boaventura, Braz Nogueira (or Texeira) and Jacques Felix. Valença Squadron
Andrade	Reserve: Maia-Marcondes region, north-west of Guará to reinforce Gaia	6th RI, Bombardas Company, a company/12th RI
Teófilo Ramos	Reserve: Matadouro Guara, right bank of Paraíba, to reinforce Sampaio	Otaviano and Inojosa Battalions

Total: 8,100 men

Federals

Eastern Army Detachment (Gen. Góis Monteiro)

(Excluding 4th Division units fighting on the Minas Gerais front)

Detachments	Composition	Strength
Daltro Filho	1st and 3rd RI, the 24th and 25th BCs, Rio Grande do Norte FP Battalion, Engineer Regiment, elements of 1st and 2nd RAM, one mountain artillery battery	7,100 soldiers
Newton Cavalcanti	19th and 23rd BCs, Bahía FP and Piaí FP Battalions, 3rd Battalion/9th RI, naval riflemen, elements of 1st GAP	3,530 soldiers
Ferreira		4,000–4,5000 soldiers
Colatino Marques	1st & 2nd/9th RI, 1st BC, 4th Battalion/Rio Grande do Sul Brigade, Sergipe FP Battalion, elements of 1st GAP	2,530 soldiers
Fontoura*	2nd RI, 3rd and 20th BCs, 2nd Battalion/Rio Grande do Sul Brigade, 4th FP Bahía Battalion, 1st GAM, elements of 1st RAM and 2nd RAM, elements of 1st GAP	4,580 soldiers
	* Departing to the Minas Front	

Total: 21,500 men

The Federal 25th BC at Barbacena. Note the absence of helmets of any type. (Arquivo Nosso Seculo, via Donato)

front of about 25–30km, being supported along their flanks by the Bocaina and Mantiqueira ranges.

In front of them, the Federal deployment was already overwhelming. For example, we have the breakdown of four major detachments of the Eastern Army. The Column Daltro Filho was made up of nine infantry battalions from 1st and 3rd RI, 24th and 25th BCs, and the Rio Grande do Norte FP Battalion, the Engineer Regiment, parts of two artillery regiments (1st and 2nd RAM) and one mountain artillery battery, that is, about 7,100 soldiers, almost matching all the Paulista forces in the area. The Column Newton Cavalcanti comprised 19th and 23rd BCs, the Bahía FP and Piaí FP Battalions, 3rd Battalion of 9th RI (from 3rd Division in the south of Brazil), the Cunha Detachment of naval riflemen from the Paulista coast and part of 1st GIAP, in total about 3,530 soldiers. The Column Colatino had the rest of 9th RI (3rd Division), 1st BC, 4th Battalion of the Rio Grande do Sul Brigade, Sergipe FP Battalion and part of 1st GIAP, adding some 2,530 personnel. Finally, there was the Column Fontoura, with 2nd RI, 3rd and 20th BCs, 2nd Battalion of the Rio Grande do Sul Brigade, the 4th FP Bahía Battalion and artillery from 1st GAM, part of 1st and 2nd RAM and elements of 1st GIAP, adding about 4,580 men.[136]. These four groups together fielded 17,440 troops, to which can be added those of a fifth detachment, the Cristóvão Ferreira, which apparently had

between 3,500 and 4,000 troops. The total Federal forces therefore comprised some 21,500 men.[137]

21–30 September: Federal Aerial Superiority

At the same time, the government's preparations for the final offensive continued. The 16 Federal combat aircraft that in theory could operate in the Paraíba were reduced to 12 on 21 September when four of them departed to Minas (Wacos number C-13 and C-17 among them), but they still apparently had eight Wacos (C-4, 'M', C-14, C-18, C-19, C-20 and C-21, plus another one), two Potezs (A-216 and A-217),

Destruction caused by the Federal bombing of Guaratinguetá by five aircraft of the so-called Bomber Platoon at the end of September (Daroz)

Amiot K-621 and NiD.72 K-422. Góis mentions only six Wacos in Resende on 22 September. Regarding the Amiot, this remained in Dos Afonsos, Rio, throughout the war, moving only to Resende on 27 September, which undoubtedly was the cause of the scarce use of this aircraft in combat missions due to the greater distance involved and crash-landing risks when flying over the Sierra de Mantiqueira.[138]

Resende Air Detachment bombed Guará and Taubaté airfields on 21 September. On 23 September, Captain Alves Seco, with Lieutenant Amarante as observer, bombed Guará with Waco C-18, which probably was unarmed as he mounted his crew members. That same day, the Bomber Platoon from Resende Air Detachment attacked Guaratinguetá with five aircraft under Lieutenants Macedo, Lavanére-Wanderley, Murici, Melo 'Maluco' and Araripe, with Major Gomes leading the group as an observer. The bombing was repeated on the 24th. Between 13 and 27 September there were also connecting flights between Resende and Lorena, and on the 25th, Melo 'Maluco' went on to reconnoitre Guará. On 26 September, Waco C-19 bombed Aparecida from the new Federal base at Lorena. Wacos C-14 and C-19 again bombed Aparecida and Guaratinguetá, while the C-21 took pictures of Paulista positions and C-18 corrected artillery shooting. On 27 September, Federal aircraft departed from Resende and made 14 bombing and reconnaissance missions over Guaratinguetá and Aparecida, landing at Cruzeiro and Lorena.[139]

In the meantime, in Rio, DH-60 Moth K-150 left Resende for Dos Afonsos on a liaison mission flown by Second Lieutenant Presser Belo, carrying Colonel Mendes Rodrigues Lima, but the aircraft crashed on take-off and was destroyed. In what proved an unfortunate decision, the colonel insisted on making the flight and departed again, this time piloting himself in the Moth registration 3003, with Captain Borges

Leitão as a companion; the aircraft crashed in the Sierra de Itaguaí, killing both occupants.[140]

Table 12: Federal Combat Aircraft on the Paraíba Front, late September 1932

Main Base: Resende

Type	Plate	Role	Notes
Waco		Fighter-Bomber	
Waco	C-14	Fighter-Bomber	
Waco	C-19	Fighter-Bomber	
Waco	C-20	Recce	Radio & camera
Waco	C-21	Recce	Radio & camera
Waco	C-4	Fighter-Bomber	
Waco	'M'	Fighter	Used for escort missions as it had synchronised machine guns
Potez	A-216	Bomber	
Potez	A-217	Bomber	
NiD.72	K-422	Fighter	
Amiot	K-621	Bomber	From Rio to Resende, 27 Sept.

Despite this incident, air operations continued. Six Wacos and a Moth departed from Resende on 28 September to seek the missing Moth, and during the same day, six other government aircraft bombed Guará and Aparecida. Finally, on 30 September, Waco C-19 coordinated with the Pouso Alegre (Minas) and Resende Air

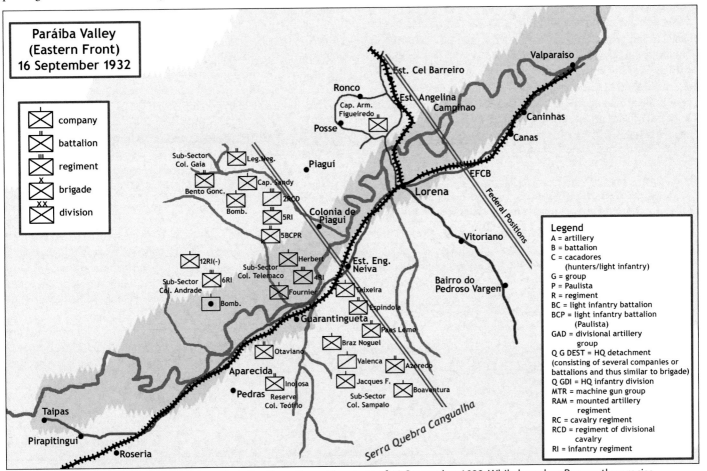

Final deployment of the Paulista units in the Guaratinguetá area, as of 18 September 1932. While based on Ramos, the precise location of every detachment is only indicative, because no good reference maps are available. The Federal Detachment Cavalcanti had enveloped all of these units while marching to the south, for Serra Cangalha and beyond. (Map by Tom Cooper)

Detachments, and again bombed Guará.[141] On 1 October, in a tricky surprise action, a government aircraft bearing Paulista aviation insignia reached and strafed Aparecida.[142]

24–29 September: The Guará Pocket

At the same time, on land, the Federals began a daily massive bombardment with artillery and aviation in preparation for the final assault on Guaratinguetá, forcing Figueiredo to evacuate civilians and send hundreds of sappers to prepare a new line of trenches further to the rear at Moreira Cesar station in Pindamonhangaba municipality.[143] Indeed, even though the Federals were somewhat weakened by the departure of Detachment Guedes Fontoura to the Minas front, their troops were sufficient and ready to move forward.[144]

The Federal Detachment Cavalcanti, from the south, tried to outflank the position of Enghneiro Neiva on the left by the Sierra de Bocaina ridge, trying to block the retreat of Paulista Detachment Sampaio to Pindamonhangaba and Taubaté, occupying Lagoinha and São Luiz do Paraitinga in the old coastal sector of Cunha and taking advantage of the evacuation of the area by the Paulistas. This advance placed the loyalists on the far left (or far south), deep in the Paulistas' rearguard, in a position to outflank even the new defensive position being prepared by Figueiredo. Consequently, it was sufficient that Cavalcanti just turn to his right (to the north), to cut the rail line and surround all the Paulista deployment. To prevent this, the rebels created a new and improvised detachment on 24 September under Lieutenant Colonel Lamego, which would cover the Jacareí–Guararema line, protecting the east of the city of São Paulo but not preventing the encirclement of Paulistas forces in Paraíba. The final offensive was put on hold by the start of talks to reach an armistice on 29 September.[145]

This was fortunate for the Paulistas because their situation was untenable and probably, had it not been for the peace talks, the war would have ended with a bloody battle of annihilation and the total destruction of the entire 2nd DIO. Surprisingly, this conclusion of the campaign, the enveloping of all Paraíba rebel positions thanks to the brilliant manoeuvre made by Cavalcanti, is not explained or mentioned by any author, although it can be deduced from the details provided by Ramos.

6
THE COASTAL FRONT

The coastal area was of secondary importance in the overall picture. Nevertheless, it had a great strategic relevance. Of primary importance was the status of the port of Santos, where imports of military equipment acquired by São Paulo during the conflict could enter, and exports of its main export asset – coffee – could leave. Understanding this, the Federals put the port under a blockade. On top of that, along the vast coast of São Paulo State the Varguistas could make landings to attack the rebel positions from behind. Although the action eventually undertaken was much more modest, as we have seen, in September it almost destroyed the whole Paulista deployment in the Paraíba Valley, which was the main concentration of rebel forces.

On the Paulista side, Santos was defended to prevent any possible landings by the 6th BCP, and later by a company of the 5th RI, as well as a company of the 6th RI and several volunteer battalions. In addition, the harbour waters were mined with improvised devices, and the 3rd GAC occupied the Itaipú Fort, bringing the total garrison of the city to about 800 soldiers, which made it very difficult to occupy by landing.[1]

The rest of the waterfront was defended by what would soon be established as a detachment under Colonel Mário Veiga Abreu, who on 17 July had, in a deployment parallel to the coast and covered by the Serra do Mar ridges, from north to south, the 3rd Company of 4th BC, two companies of 1st BCP and three machine-gun sections in Cunha; to the south-west, in São Luiz do Paraitinga, part of a company of 4th BC and a machine-gun section; further south-west, in Paraibuna, a company of 1st BCP, and at Galeopolis the 1st Platoon of 4th BC, both guarding the distant Naval Air Station at São Sebastião Island; and as a reserve in Taubaté, towards the centre of the deployment – but about 40km further back – along the Rio–São Paulo railway, a company of 4th BC and a machine-gun section.[2] In total, about 800 soldiers were divided into small garrisons each of about 100 men, except Cunha, which comprised half of the entire contingent.

10–15 July 1932: Blockade and Bombardment of Santos

The first major action by the Federals was the departure, between 10 and 11 July, of 1st Naval Division – the cruiser *Rio Grande do Sul* and anti-torpedo boats or destroyers *Mato Grosso*, *Pará* and *Sergipe* – from the port of Rio de Janeiro to blockade Santos. The blockade proved a success, with only one rebel ship managing to leave the port during the war, on 12 July, bringing in coffee and obtaining foreign currency worth US$150,000.[3] To support the blockade and protect them from air strikes, three fast SM-55 A seaplanes, with number plates 1, 4 and 8, piloted by Frigate Captain Antonio Augusto Schorcht, Corbette Captain Epaminondas Santos and Captain-Lieutenant Braulio Gouvê, departed from the Naval Air base at Galeão, Rio. These heavy Savoia hydroplanes could carry 2,000kg of bombs,

Location	Detachment	Composition	Strength
Santos		6th BCP; later company/5th RI, company/6th RI, volunteer battalions, 3rd GAC	800 soldiers, 8 cannons
Cunha	Veiga Abreu	3rd Company/4th BC, 2 companies/1st BCP, 3 machine-gun sections	400 soldiers
South-west: São Luiz do Paraitinga	Veiga Abreu	Half company/4th BC, machine-gun section	100 soldiers
Blocking Naval Air Station at São Sebastiao Island: Paraibuna & Gaelopolis	Veiga Abreu	One company/1st BCP, 1st Platoon/4th BC	150 soldiers
Reserve: Taubaté	Veiga Abreu	One company/4th BC, machine-gun section	150 soldiers
Total			**1,600 soldiers**

Table 13: Paulista Forces on the Coastal Sector, 17 July 1932

Table 14: Federal Forces Blocking Santos, 10–12 July 1932

1st Naval Division

Cruiser *Rio Grande do Sul*	
Destroyer *Mato Grosso*	
Destroyer *Pará*	
Destroyer *Sergipe*	

Naval Aviation

Vila Vela, São Sebastiao Island

Type	Plate Number
SM-55 A	1
SM-55 A	4
SM-55 A	8
Martin	111
Martn	112

1st Observation Division (Naval)

Galeao Naval Base, Rio de Janeiro

Capt. Petit

Corsair	1-0-2
Corsair	1-0-3
Corsair	1-0-4
Corsair	1-0-6

yet reached speeds of 280km/h, while their Paulista rivals barely managed 210–215km/h.[4] The Federal seaplanes could therefore escape from them easily without needing an escort, unless their foes were at a higher altitude and could dive to gain speed in an attack. In addition, two Martin PM seaplanes, numbered 111 and 112, departed under Captain-Lieutenants Ismael Brazil and Reynalod de Carvalho. Unlike the Savoias, these were much slower, with a speed of just 184km/h, and were therefore easy prey for any rebel aviation in the area. These five Federal seaplanes landed on the island of São Sebastião, in Ilhabela, about 80km inside the border of São Paulo and only some 100km from Santos. They were able to be based here despite the rough waters around the island as their large size made them more stable.[5]

On 12 July, the three Savoias, numbered 1, 4 and 8, conducted a reconnaissance flight over Santos. They repeated the operation the next day, but came under anti-aircraft artillery fire from Fort Itaipú and some cannons based at Monte Serrat. In retaliation, the Savoias attacked the area with 15 bombs, damaging the electrical installations of the 1st Battery of the 3rd GAC.[6] At the same time, the Varguistas took advantage of the ensuing confusion and a destroyer tried to enter the harbour, only to be forced back by coastal artillery.[7]

15–17 July 1932: The Federal Landing

On 15 July, the first ground operation in this theatre began when the government Naval Fusiliers Detachment landed in Paraty, a salient on the westernmost tip of Rio de Janeiro State that penetrated deeply into São Paulo State, and from which one could move towards Cunha and, after crossing the Serra do Mar, attack the rear of all the rebel forces in the Paraíba Valley.[8] Indeed, from Cunha to Guaratinguetá (where the railroad and the Rio–São Paulo road joined, and which was the main supply route for 2nd DIO) was only 55km, connected by a good road. Other roads led from Cunha to Campos Novos and Lorena in the east and Lagoinha and São Luiz do Paratinga (defended

A pair of Martin PM 1-B seaplanes, with several SM-55s in the background, at the Ilhabela air base on São Sebastião island. (SDM via Sergio Luis dos Santos)

A Naval Martin PM 1-B seaplane at the Ilhabela base. (Daróz)

by a company of the 4th BC) in the west, also threatening São Jose dos Campos, Jacari and, eventually, the Paulista capital. For this reason, foreseeing the Federal advance on 13 July, the rebels took the lead and occupied Cunha with a company of 4th BC and a machine-gun section. On the 14th, another company and a section of 1st BCP arrived, followed two days later by a further company of the same battalion. Assuming the command of the improvised Veiga Abreu Detachment, Major Ribeiro dos Santos had at his disposal about 360 soldiers, near half of all the rebel deployment in the area.[9]

At dawn the next day, government fusilier patrols from Parati clashed for the first time with the Paulistas outside Cunha, resulting in the government troops being captured. The Federal assault on the town began that afternoon. Although according to Silva the government detachment led by Captain João Alberto included

Rebel officers checking the damage to Fort Itaipú after the Federal bombardment. (Daróz)

Detachment, created officially on 15 July, also included a two-piece artillery section.[11]

In support of this offensive, the Naval Aviation performed several missions from 16–18 July, including a reconnaissance sortie over Cunha on the 17th, two Corsairs departing from Galeão, Rio, trying without success to locate the Paulista artillery operating in the sector.[12] That same day, a Federal seaplane dropped leaflets over Santos, but while returning it had an engine failure and had to land in the sea at Queimada Grande, still far from its base at Ilhabela. Although several witnesses, including a merchant ship, stated that it was sunk, the fact is that no aircraft was registered as lost on this day, so the seaplane must have eventually made it back. The Paulistas reacted by sending a Waco from Lorena to bomb the loyalist positions around Cunha on 17 July. On 18 July, two Federal

the Naval Fusiliers, a Federal District FP battalion and another from Espírito Santo, on the contrary, Ramos and Donato state that it consisted of only 500 soldiers from the Naval Fusiliers.[10] The Cunha

A campaign telephone in the Cunha trenches. (Museo da Imagem e do Som, São Paulo, via Donato)

Paulista poet Guilherme de Almeida, with the cigarette, and Roque, in Cunha. Roque was a clown in 2nd Division about whom there are few details, it is not clear if he was a mascot for the division. (Museu da Imagem e do Som, São Paulo, via Donato)

Detail of the pilot and machine-gun position of Federal Navy Vought Corsair 1-0-2. Note the pirate drawing on the textile cover of the fuselage. This aircraft was involved in the suppression of rebel artillery support and supply in the coastal region. (Daróz)

A detailed view of the bomb racks of a Martin PM 1-B seaplane, probably being armed for a mission at the Ilhabela base. The machine gun has not still been installed in the ring in the nose. (SDM via Sergio Luis dos Santos)

a direct hit on a wagon full of ammunition, causing a huge explosion.[14]

The Varguistas launched their assault on Cunha on 19 July. The rebel defenders, formed by two companies of 4th BC and another two from 1st BCP, were in positions outside the city, in the Morro del Divino Mestre. Federal forces surrounded the left flank of their positions, supported by a section of light machine guns, forcing 30 Paulistas from the platoon defending that sector to retreat. The government units then approached the town, whose panicked population fled. Consequently, the rebel troops had to retreat at full speed to defend the city. In these battles, the well-known Brazilian poet Guilherme de Almeida had his baptism of fire. By the 20th, the Naval Fusiliers were almost inside Cunha, advancing at bayonet-point. However, the machine-gun section of 1st BCP that arrived as reinforcement the previous day from Guará was able to place a gun with eight soldiers in an elevated position and for three hours poured fire on the attackers, who finally retreated. Despite the duration of the combat, the Paulistas suffered only one dead, while the Federals lost one killed, three officers and several sailors taken prisoner, and 15 wounded.[15]

The next day, 21 July, there was another air strike made by two Corsairs under Petit, again attacking at low altitude against supposed rebel artillery positions, bombarding them

Corsairs again took off from Galeão, but they were unable to locate an enemy battery, although they did see 100 rebel soldiers in a column of trucks. The land forces fired on the Federal aircraft and hit that of First Lieutenant Khal Filho, who managed to return to base.[13]

19–21 July: The First Federal Assault on Cunha

The damage to Khal's aircraft must have been light, for on the next day, 19 July, he departed again – with all the available Corsairs of the 1st Observation Division (1-0-2, 1-0-3, 1-0-4 and 1-0-6) – to repeat the mission. This time they were divided into two sections of two aircraft each, flying at just 13 metres high, until they found a convoy of wagons pulled by horses and oxen on the edge of a forest. The rebels opened fire as soon as they saw the aircraft approaching, but the pilots pressed home their attack, releasing 15kg bombs, one of which scored

successfully. Petit then proceeded to strafe Paulista soldiers found along the way. In this action, Lieutenant Oriano Menescal, piloting the other aircraft, refused to open fire, arguing that he had departed to destroy the enemy artillery and not to shoot some poor scared soldiers who were running away.[16]

24 July – 12 August: Strategic Bombing and the Littoral Air Forces

Meanwhile, the Varguistas managed to finish the Ilhabela airfield on São Sebastião island on 24 July, and Petit's Corsairs from 1st Observation Division were deployed there, halfway between Santos and Cunha and therefore within easy reach of both fronts, leaving their distant base at Galeão in Rio.[17]

Federal SM-55 plate number 1. The unusual design of the Savoia, with its twin tails, double fuselage and twin motors with propellers in front and behind are evident in this picture. This model made the first strategic bombing in the Western Hemisphere, and was the first to cross the South Atlantic. (Daróz)

Captain Djalma Petit, commander of the Federal 1st Division of Observation, of four Corsair aircraft. (Daróz)

Ever since 13 July, Góis Monteiro had planned to bomb the Paulistas' ammunition factories, run by the Matarazzo Group, in the first instance of strategic bombing in the Americas, followed later by attacks on the gas-oil deposits of the rebels, but had been opposed by the Chief of Staff, Tasso Fragoso. He argued that in any escalation of the conflict, the rebels might use toxic gas. Brazil was also at this

time in Geneva defending the prohibition of bombing civilian objectives. Faced with the threat of Fragoso's resignation on 26 July, Góis was forced to change tactics, and suggested instead the bombing of power plants rather than rebel industry to leave the Paulista factories without light, and therefore unable to produce.[18]

Therefore, on 27 July the Federals flew the first 'strategic' bombing mission in the entire American continent. Two Savoia-Marchetti SM-55 seaplanes and a Martin PM took off from Ilhabela to bomb the Cubatão Light Company power plant near Santos. They were escorted by two Corsairs. The mission had to be aborted due to engine failure of one of the Savoias, but the Martin PM continued, unaware of the cancellation, until 20 minutes from its goal. Then, noticing the absence of the Corsairs and the Savoias, it too returned to base. The Corsairs, however, had been at their meeting point, but 600 metres higher than the Martin, who could not see them. The next day, 28 July, they once again launched a Savoia and a Martin, escorted by two Corsairs, but they could not carry out the attack because the target was covered with clouds. Finally, later that morning – or the next day – the Savoia managed to drop a 68kg bomb, but it did not hit the target due to bad weather and poor visibility.[19]

At the same time, the government took the opportunity to better organise the deployed forces on the island of São Sebastião. Apart from the four Corsairs of the 1st Division of Observation under Petit, grouped into two sections, they created the Littoral Air Defence Force, led by Captain Schorcht. This unit, despite its name, was not a force of fighters, but of bombers and reconnaissance seaplanes. It was organised as follows: captaincy, Savoia SM-55 number 1; 1st Section, Martin numbers 111 and 112; 2nd Section, Savoia numbers 4 and 8; 3rd Section, Moth observation aircraft numbers 1-1-2, 1-1-6 and 1-1-10; 4th Section, Moth numbers 1-1-1, 1-1-7 and 1-1-9. In addition, Savoia numbers 6, 10 and 11 would be incorporated later, perhaps as an additional section, but for the moment they were repairing in Rio. The Moths, light unarmed airplanes with a top speed of only 135km/h compared to the 210–215km/h of the Paulistas, were limited to ground recce and support missions in three-aircraft sections, one aircraft equipped with a machine gun, one with bombs and another with a radio.[20]

On 30 July, one of the Corsairs was diverted to serve in the Paraíba Valley, at the Resende base.[21] The next day, although the Paulistas had no combat aircraft in the area they did have civilian aircraft carrying out occasional liaison missions, transportation and recognition. A Laté 26 from the French company Aeropostal, that had been requisitioned in Praia Grande by the rebels to work as a transport, was observed near the island of São Sebastião. A Corsair piloted by First Lieutenant Buarque de

Table 15: Forces involved in the Second Battle of Cunha, 10–26 August 1932		
Paulistas		
Detachment	**Composition**	**Strength**
Ribeiro	3rd Company/4th BC, 2 companies/1st BCP, 3 machine-gun sections	400 soldiers
Ribeiro (19 Aug. reinforcements)	2 mixed companies, 4th, 5th, 8th BCPs, 2 companies/General Osorio Battalion	800 soldiers
Total		**1,200 soldiers, 1 cannon**
Federals		
Nelson de Melo	Naval Fusiliers, Federal District FP, Espírito Santo FP Battalions, artillery	1,600–1,700 men and artillery

Lima took off to down it, but the rebel unit managed to escape through the clouds.[22]

10–26 August: The Paulista Victory at Cunha

On the inland front, although their initial assault had been repelled, the Federalists maintained their positions blockading the city of Cunha. After receiving artillery on 30 July, they began bombing the town, and launched a further infantry assault to overwhelm the rebel left flank on 10 August. The attack was led by Captain Nelson de Melo, who had replaced Alberto on 30 July. Silva mentions up to 2,000 Federal troops involved in the attack, but there were probably about 1,500 plus some artillery, comprising the previously mentioned Naval Fusiliers, Federal District FP and Espírito Santo FP battalions. Despite getting to within 150 metres of the rebel positions, the government attack was repulsed once more. They resumed their attack on 11 August, with artillery support and naval aviation, and the final assault occurred on 15 August after firing 115 shells over a period of three hours, compared to a mere five rounds from the rebel cannons on the left flank. On the eastern flank, the Federals occupied Roça Grande, and on

Damage caused by air strikes on the 1st Battery of 3rd GAC in Fort Itaipú. (Daróz)

The surviving Martin PM 1-B seaplane after the war at Galeão, with post-war number plate GM-P-10. It was probably numbered 111 during the conflict. (SDM via Sergio Luis dos Santos)

the right one, after the rebels ran out of ammunition, they took Usina, just 5km from the town. The bombardment continued on the 16th, with 60 projectiles fired at rebel positions. Due to bad weather, Federal air support disappeared between 15 and 20 August. The trenches on the left flank, defended by 1st BCP, suffered five wounded from the bombing; with morale plummeting due to ammunition stocks being exhausted, Ribeiro began to organise a withdrawal. However, no final Federal attack came. Thus, that night the Paulista troops received fresh ammunition, and reinforcements were requested from the garrisons of Campos Novos and Lagoinha.[23]

In any case, the moment of greatest danger had passed. On 19 August, Major Ribeiro received two mixed companies of the 4th, 5th and 8th BCPs, under the command of Major Monteiro, and two others from the 'General Osorio' Battalion under Captain Romancio, which increased the garrison at Cunha to some 1,200 or 1,400 men. Ribeiro organised a brilliantly executed counter-attack with his whole force. He deployed his troops on both Federal flanks in Campos Novos and Usina, and launched his attack at dawn on 20 August, maintaining the pressure until the 25th, occupying the Divino Mestre ridge and the loyalists pushing out of all their positions, who fled towards Paratí. The Paulistas advanced some 15–20km, killing 60 Federals and wounding

many more. They seized the Federal supplies and took 100,000 rounds of ammunition. Following their defeat, the government troops retreated to the base of the Sierra de Parati ridge, between São Paulo and Rio, and there entrenched themselves. They never threatened Cunha again. Once the danger was over, the Paulistas' reinforcements returned to Guaratinguetá.[24] This brilliant defensive action, with its successful use and deployment of the reserves, gives an idea of how the Paulistas could have acted on the other fronts, profiting from their central position to reinforce the most endangered position and launch aggressive counter-attacks, and then returning these troops to other sectors. Yet sadly for the Paulistas, this operation proved the exception and not the rule.

8 August and 12 September: Air Battles over Santos

Noting the absence of the UAC, the Federals redeployed some of their combat aircraft to other front lines. Either sometime between 8 and 10 August, or on 12 August, two Corsairs commanded by Petit and three DH.60 Moths departed for the south. On 20 August, another Corsair was sent in the same direction, but that aircraft was destroyed in a crash near Jacarezinho.[25] This left the Littoral Air Force supported by just one Corsair, and indeed it seems this service was down to only nine aircraft during September: a Corsair, two Martins (registrations 111 and 112) and six Savoias (registrations 1, 4, 6, 8, 10 and 11), of which two were undergoing repairs at Galeão.[26]

This was the force that, from 3 September, opened an aerial offensive on the port of Santos. Requiring no escort, thanks to their speed, three Savoias (1, 6, and 11) launched from Ilhabela to bombard the 3rd GAC's positions at the entrance to the harbour. Due to the high altitude that was required to avoid ground fire only five of their 68kg bombs scored hits, causing minimal damage. In turn, the Paulistas claimed one of bombers as damaged. Two days later, on 5 September, three Savoias – supposedly escorted by two Martins (although it is unclear how the latter keep up with the much faster bombers) – unleashed a total of 1,180kg of bombs upon the Paulista artillery: the 1st Battery of 3rd GAC in Fort Itaipú was completely obliterated, while the 2nd Battery was heavily damaged, as were the electric installations of the fort. While this was one of most successful air strikes of the war, the Federalists did not know that almost no guns were left in the fort: most had been removed early on during the war and were meanwhile installed on armoured trains on several battlefields. Thus, their bombs pulverised mainly only cardboard decoys.[27]

Convinced they had caused decisive damage, the Federals then deployed their fast amphibious aircraft for daily flights over Santos to drop newspapers and leaflets in an attempt to lower rebel morale. Such operations came to a sudden end when they came under fire from guns at Fort Itaipú on 9 September, and thereafter new air strikes were launched against this facility. On 12 September, a storm forced the crew of one Martin (112) to make an emergency landing at sea: when a tugboat attempted to tow it back to Ilhabela, the aircraft sank in the São Sebastião Channel.[28]

16–24 September: The First Naval Anti-Aircraft Artillery Downing in the Western Hemisphere

The air battle for Santos came to an abrupt end on 24 September, when the Paulistas – after realising that the Federalists had only one fighter aircraft active in the area – deployed the UAC in an all-out attempt at breaking the blockade of the port. However, all their intercept attempts failed due to the superior speed of the Savoias. Thereafter, the five Paulista aircraft flew ground strikes in the Cunha sector.[29]

For these operations, the rebels also intended to deploy the requisitioned civil Laté 26, adapted to carry six 90kg bombs. However, this suffered an engine failure prior to take-off. The other aircraft – including the Falcons *Kyri-Kyri* (flown by Major Lysias Rodriguez, with Second Lieutenant Pereira de Almeida as observer), *Kavuré-Y* (with Captain Gomes Ribeiro and his friend and lawyer, Second Lieutenant Machado Bittencourt) – took off without a problem and approached their target at an altitude of 1,600m, accompanied by the *Waco Verde* flown by Captain Motta Filho.[30]

The intention of the attack was not so much to destroy 1st Naval Division, but to distract it sufficiently to allow the entry into the harbour of the freighter SS *Ruth*, carrying vital supplies for the war. Towards noon on 24 September, the three Paulista aircraft arrived over Santos and identified the cruiser *Rio Grande do Sul* near Moela Island, the main ship of the Federal fleet, moored along the bar. The Scout-class cruiser weighed 3,000 tons, was 122 metres long and had a top speed of 25 knots.[31] It was heavily armed, with ten 120mms guns, six 47mm guns, two torpedo tubes and two Hotchkiss anti-aircraft machine guns that had been taken from the submarine *Humaitá*, so it was a tough nut to crack. Despite this, Major Lysias valiantly began an attack on the ship. However, the first to dive was *Kavuré-Y* under Gomes Ribeiro, which dropped a series of bombs that splintered the deck of the cruiser and wounded two sailors. However, almost simultaneously the aircraft exploded into a huge fireball, killing both the pilot and Machado Bittencourt, which tragically brought an end to their adventure which had started two months previously when they escaped from Rio dressed as fishermen to join the São Paulo aviation.[32]

It is unclear whether the aircraft was shot down by anti-aircraft artillery or its loss was the result of an accident. According to the testimony of

Table 16: Aviation in the Coastal Sector, August–September 1932				
Federal Littoral Air Force				
Frigate Captain Antonio Augusto Schorcht				
Ilhabela airfield, São Sebastião island				
Unit	**Type**	**Plate Number**	**Arrival**	**Departing**
Captaincy	SM-55	1		
Section 1	Martin	111		
	Martin	112		12 Sept, sunk by accident
Section 2	SM-55	4		
	SM-55	8		
Section 3	Moth	1-1-2		1st week Sept, to RGS
	Moth	1-1-6		1st week Sept, to RGS
	Moth	1-1-10		1st week Sept, to RGS
Section 4	Moth	1-1-1		1st week Sept, to RGS
	Moth	1-1-7		1st week Sept, to RGS
	Moth	1-1-9		1st week Sept, to RGS
Section 5	SM-55	6	3 Sept	
	SM-55	10		
	SM-55	11	3 Sept	
1st Observation Division				
Capt. Djalma Petit (departing 8–12 Aug)				
	Corsair	1-0-2	24 July	* See note
	Corsair	1-0-3	24 July	* See note
	Corsair	1-0-4	24 July	8–12 Aug, to the south
	Corsair	1-0-6	24 July	8–12 Aug, to the south
* Note: 3 Moths departed, and 1 additional Corsair was sent to the south, being lost in an accident on 20 Aug.				

The cruiser *Rio Grande do Sul*, one of the Federal components of the 1st Naval Division blockade of Santos. It was attacked by two Paulista Falcons and a Waco, probably destroying one of the former with its anti-aircraft artillery, perhaps being the first downing in this category in the Americas. (Daróz)

Francisco Amaro, it was First Class Seaman Raynol who fired the Hotchkiss that hit the aircraft and brought it down. On the other hand, Major Lysias says its loss was the product of an accident because Gomes Ribeiro, against the advice of Lysias, had dived with the engine at full capacity, which caused a valve to become jammed and produce a flame which blew up the engine. Another explanation, according to Ivo Borges, was that the explosion occurred due to the use of potassium chloride, an unstable explosive.

The authors who defend the accident thesis argue that if the aircraft had been shot down by artillery fire, this should have hit the Green Waco first, as it was flying 200 metres below, not the Falcon. However, this argument does not stand up to scrutiny as the Hotchkiss bullets could have missed the first aircraft but then continued their path to strike the next one. On the other hand, Amaro claimed that the downed aircraft had made an earlier attack, and it was on its second run that it was engulfed in flames. Perhaps the first one was not the same aircraft but the other Falcon or the Waco. Whatever the case, all the other bombs missed their target.[33] If it is true that the Falcon was indeed shot down, it would have been the first downing of an aircraft by naval anti-aircraft artillery in the Western Hemisphere. Whatever the case, the incident ended the Paulistas' operations on the coast and the air

Table 17: Paulista Anti-Ship Task Force, 24 September 1932

Campo de Marte, São Paulo

Type	Plate Number	Fate
Laté 26		Cancelled due to engine failure
Falcon	*Kiry-Kiry*	
Falcon	*Kavuré-Y*	Downed by anti-aircraft artillery or accident
Waco	C-3 *Verde*	

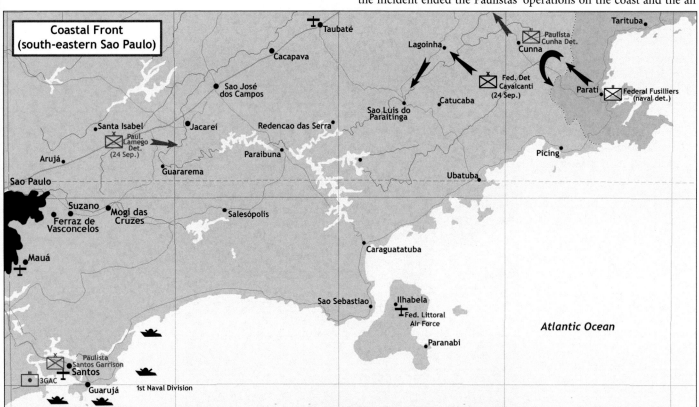

A map of the Coastal Front during the war. In this area, most of the fighting was concentrated in the Cunna/Cunha area, and the air and naval blockade of the port of Santos. In September 1932, the Cunha detachment of the Paulistas withdrew while the Federal Cavalcanti Detachment ran its enveloping manoeuvre through the emerging gap in the front line to reach São Luiz do Paraitinga. (Map by Tom Cooper)

The two Paulista pilots killed in the attack on the cruiser *Rio Grande do Sul*: Captain Jose Agnelo Gomes Ribeiro, right, and Lieutenant Mário Machado Bittencourt. Bittencourt was a lawyer and amateur aviator, who joined Ribeiro due to their friendship. They are seen in front of a rebel Waco, but the aircraft they used to attack the ship was a Falcon. (Daróz).

battle for Santos.

The next day, 25 September, the Paulistas made a desperate attempt to incorporate a new aircraft into its fleet. A Panair passenger Sikorsky S-38 in Rio, registration number P-BDAD, was hijacked by two mechanics and a pilot, who deceived the watchman that guarded it. It appears that the aircraft then took off under mechanic Jaime Taveira. However, when it was only 20km from Rio, it seems that the guard, Manoel Machado, realised that they were trying to defect to São Paulo and so began a struggle, which resulted in the aircraft crashing and everyone aboard being killed.[34]

12–29 September: The Paulista Collapse on the Coast

The news on the ground was no better for the Paulistas. Although the victory in Cunha provided them with a few weeks' respite, the successive withdrawals in the Paraíba Valley and the lack of troops to cover all the sectors resulted in an order for 1st BCP to fall back to Guaratinguetá on 12 September, from where the unit was redeployed to Campinas on the Minas front. Captain O'Reilly from 4th BC assumed command of the Cunha sector, but withdrew from the city to the Serra da Quebra Cangalha ridge, covering the far right of Sampaio Detachment, in the Paraíba Valley, from 16–18 September.[35]

Although no author mentions it, this retreat was a terrible mistake as it left the entire coastal region south of the Paraíba Valley entirely defenceless. The Federal Newton Cavalcanti Detachment, in the

An impressive Paulista poster published by the MMDC Militia as a call for recruitment, inspired by the well-known 'Uncle Sam needs You' poster. This is the most famous graphic document of the 1932 war. The legend in Brazilian Portuguese says: "You have a duty to fulfill. Check with your conscience". Sadly, the artist remains unknown. Notable is the Adrian helmet of the soldier, and the Paulista flag in the background. (Donato)

southern part of the government's position, slipped through the hole and moved west around the rebel position in Guaratinguetá, and assuming command of the Federal Cunha Detachment it continued its advance, taking Lagoinha and São Luiz do Paraitinga. The Paulistas attempted to fill this gap with the creation of a new Detachment Lamego for the area of Jacareí–Guararema, but this was insufficient because although it could protect the access east of São Paulo city, it could do nothing to prevent the envelopment of the rebel 2nd Division made by Cavalcanti in its rear.[36] Luckily for the Paulistas, the armistice prevented this last battle from being fought.

BIBLIOGRAPHY

(All in Brazilian unless stated otherwise)

Books.

Anom. *Historia do Exercito Brasileiro* (Brasília: Estado Maior do Exercito, 1972)

Apolinário, Eric Lucian, *Inverno Escarlate* (São Paulo: Editora Gregory, 2018)

Coutinho, Lourival, *O General Goes Depoe* (Rio de Janeiro: Coelho Branco, 1956)

Daróz, Carlos Roberto Carvalho, (I) *Un Céu Cinzento* (Rio de Janeiro: Biblioteca do Exercito, 2017)

Donato, Hernani, (I) *A Revolução de 32* (São Paulo: Circulo do Livro, 1982)

Donato, Hernani, (II) *Dicionário das Batalhas Brasileiras* (São Paulo: Ibrasa, 1996)

Flores Jr, Jackson, *Aeronaves Militares Brasileiras* (Rio de Janeiro: Action Editora, 2016)

Garcia da Silveira, Ronan, *Historia de Coxim* (Coxim: Prefeitura de Coxim, 1995)

Giorgis, Caminha, Luiz Eduardo, *Historia de la III Region Militar, Volume II* (Porto Alegre: Unknown Publisher)

Hagedorn, Dan, *Latin American Air Wars 1912–1969* (Crowborough: Hikoki Publications, 2006) (English)

Hilton, Stanley, *1932, A Guerra Civil Brasileira* (Rio de Janeiro: NovaFronteira, 1982)

Ibanhes, Brígido, *Selvino Jacques, o último dosbandoleiros* (S. Paulo: Scortecci Editora, 1995)

Iglesias, Francisco, *Historia Contemporánea de Brasil* (Mexico: Fondo de Cultura Económica, 1999) (Spanish)

Jowett, Philip, *Latin American Wars 1900–1941* (Oxford: Osprey, 2018) (English)

McCann, Frank, *Soldiers of the Pátria* (Stanford: Stanford University Press, 2003) (English)

Paraná do Brasil, Irany, *1932, a Guerra de São Paulo* (São Paulo: Factash Editoria, 2006)

Passos, Rodolpho Emiliano, *Goiás de ontem* (Goiana: Author's edition, 1987)

Pereira Leite Neto, Luiz, *As Operaçoes Militares na Revolução de 1932* (Rio de Janeiro: Monografia Escola de Comando e Estado Maior do Exercito, ECEME, 1991)

Peres Zanetti, Sandro, *Intervenção do Exército no proceso político Brasileiro* (Rio de Janeiro: Escola de Comando e Estado Maior do Exercito Mareschal Castello Branco, 2009)

Puigari, Umberto, *Nas Fronteiras de Mato Grosso, Terra Abandonada* (São Paulo: Umberto Puigari, 1933)

Ramos, Antonio, *As Operaçoes Militares na Revolução de 1932* (Rio de Janeiro: Monografia ECEME, 1989)

Rodrigues, Jose Wasth and Barroso, Gustavo, *Uniformes do Exercito Brasileiro, 1730–1922* (Rio de Janeiro: Ministerio de Guerra,1922)

Silva, Herculano de Carvalho, *A Revolução Constitucionalista* (São Paulo: Civilização Brasileira, 1932)

Articles

Cotta, Francis Albert, ´As Trincheras da Mantiqueira´, Policia Militar de Minas Gerais, 2017 <https://revista.policiamilitar.mg.gov.br/index.php/alferes/article/view/120>, accessed 2017

Daróz, Carlos Roberto Carvalho, (II) ´Aviação de caça e pesca?´, *ll Seminario de Estudos: Poder Aeroespacial e Estudis Estrategicos* (Programa de Pos-graduacão em Ciencias Aeroespaciales – UNIFA, 2009)

(III) `O Fantasma Da Morte – O Trem Blindado Paulista de 1932´, Daroz Historia Militar (2010) < https://darozhistoriamilitar.blogspot.com/2010/05/o-fantasma-da-morte-o-trem-blindado.html?_sm_au_=iVV61S07NsGGnJWFj1q0vKscFs0qW>, accessed 2018

Della Rosa, Ricardo, ´A Frente do Vale do Paraíba na Revolução de 1932´, *Jornal o Lince* (2010), <http://www.jornalolince.com.br/2010/arquivos/panopticum-frente-vale-paraiba-revolucao-1932-www.jornaolince.com.br-edicao033.pdf>, accessed 2018

García de Gabiola, Javier, `Sao Paulo en armas´, *Historia y Vida nº 535* (Barcelona: Prisma, 2012) (Spanish)

Helio Lopes, Raimundo, 'Entre Militares e voluntarios: Os Batalhoes Provisorios cearenses', *Revista Brasileira de Historia Militar*, Ano 1, n 2, agosto 2010. RBHMh

Juncal, Fabriciano, `Batalhoes de Araçatuba´, Museu Araça (2017) <http://museuaraca.blogspot.de/p/ata-e-revolucao-de-32.html>, accessed 2017

Lintz Geraldo, Alcyr, ` Aviação no Conflito Constitucionalista de 1932´, Reservaer (2008), <http://reservaer.com.br>, accessed 2017

Maranhão, Ricardo, `São Paulo 1932, Tecnología a Serviço da Revolução´, Netleland (2008) <http://netleland.net/hasampa/epopeia1932/rev32tech.html>, accessed 2017

Moreira Bento, Claudio (I), `Operaçoes da Aviação do Exercito a partir de Resende, no combate a Revolução de 1932 no Vale de Paraíba e frente Mineira´, Docplayer (2018), <https://docplayer.com.br/51398963-Operacoes-da-aviacao-do-exercito-a-partir-de-resende-no-combate-a-revolucao-de-1932-no-vale-do-Paraíba-e-frente-mineira.html>, accessed 2018

(II) `Os 70 Anos da Revolução Paulista de 1932´, *O Guararapes*. CGC 10.149.526/0001-09 (2009), n 35, Oct-Dec.

Ribeiro, Arnor da Silva, ´Mundos de Silvino Jacques´, Theses and Dissertations, São Paulo University (2011) <https://teses.usp.br>, accessed 2018

Ribeiro, Cassio, `A Revolução Constitucionalista de 1932´, O Rebate (2008), < http://orebate-cassioribeiro.blogspot.com/2008/07/revoluo-constitucionalista-de-1932.html?_sm_au_=iVV61S07NsGGnJWFj1q0vKscFs0qW>, accessed 2016

Righi, Sérgio, ´O Estado de Maracajú e o Movimento Constitucionalista de 1932´, Ultima Trincheira (2018) < http://www.ultimatrincheira.com.br/maracaju.htm>, accessed 2018

Silva Parreira, Luiz Eduardo:
(i) `E o Sul do Mato Grosso foi às Armas!`,*Polemologia* (2012) <https://polemologia.blogspot.com>, accessed 2019
(ii) `*Tres Lagoas: O front esquecido da Revoluçao de 32 no sul do Mato Grosso*´. Unpublished (2019)

Soares, Fidelis Julio Cesar, `Calibre 32. Resende em Armas´,
    Universidad Foral Ruiz de Fora, ECSB Defesa (2010) <http://
    www.ecsbdefesa.com.br/defesa/fts/CALIBRE32.pdf>,
    accessed 2017

Walsh, Paul P., `*The Paulista War: An Example of Conventional
    Warfare in Latin America in the Inter-War Period´,* Conference
    held at the Military History Society (Calgary: Unpublished,
    2002) (English)

Web Pages

Dell Rosa, Ricardo, <www.tudoporSãopaulo.com.br>, Collectable
    web page, now moved to Facebook, accessed 2016
<www.desastresaereos.net>
<Jusbrasil.com.br>
LAAHS: Latin American Aviation Historical Society, <http://
    laahs.com>
<Naval.com.br>
<www.revolvy.com>
<www.rudnei.cunha.nom.br>

NOTES

Chapter 1
1   It had actually been completed on 31 October 1931.
2   In 1932 the Samba Schools were introduced into the parade for the first time, which gave the Carnival its current colour and flavour.
3   Iglesias, pp. 17–48. Donato, p. 19. García de Gabiola, p. 62.
4   Iglesias, pp. 51–68. García de Gabiola, pp. 62–63.
5   Hilton, p. 39. Ribeiro, pp. 3–5. García de Gabiola, p. 63.
6   Hilton, pp. 66, 72–81. García de Gabiola, p. 63.

Chapter 2
1   No single source provides a complete order of battle of the Brazilian Army for the period in question. Most details were thus prepared on the basis of Decree No. 13,916 of 11 December 1919 and No. 15,235 of 31 December 1921, available at www.jusbrasil.com.br. Further details are from García de Gabiola, pp. 63–64. Moreover, Rodrigues (pp. 72–74) has been used to deduce the order of battle of the Brazilian Army in 1932 and the deployment location of every unit. Finally, the deployment of some regiments from 2nd and 4th Divisions has been deduced from several narratives of the 1932 combats and from Della Rosa's web page.
2   Article 7 of Decree 15,235 of 31 December 1921.
3   Article 9 of Decree 15,235 of 31 December 1921. Three groups were established per regiment, but Article 21 provided that the third group would be formed later.
4   Article 10 of Decree 15,235 of 31 December 1921.
5   Decree No. 15,235 of 31 December 1921 created the divisions in Article 2 and set the units that composed them. Also, it provided for the constitution of two infantry brigades and one heavy artillery regiment per division to be created later, but these has not been formed by 1932. Similarly, it anticipated a heavy artillery regiment per division that never existed. Article 21 stated that the 2nd and 3rd Artillery Group of these regiments would not be formed, only the 1st. This would become an independent group of heavy artillery or GIAP within every division and probably took the same number as the parent unit.
6   Article 21 of Decree 15,235 of 31 December 1921. Daróz, p. 108. Decree 13,652 of 18 June 1919.

    For example, 10th RAM is mentioned in the regulations, but in a later article, it is stated that it would not be activated for the moment, however, there is evidence of it fighting in Mantiqueira and so it must have been activated during the war. On the other hand, 3rd RAM, which should have been part of the rebel Paulista 2nd Division, is not mentioned in any source, so it is likely that sometime between 1921 and 1932 it was decided that the regiment would be not created, or it was suppressed from the records. Similarly, 4th RI, under 2nd Division, despite being mentioned, would not be activated according to the 1921 regulation, but this criterion must have been changed as this unit is later mentioned amongst the Paulista units. Concerning the mountain artillery groups (*Montanha*), although it was determined that 2nd, 3rd and 4th were not going to be activated, we know from Daróz that at least the 2nd was organised in 1932. Finally, 14th and 15th IR/5th Division are not mentioned in any sources about the war. As we know that in the 1919 regulation it was determined that these three units (13th, 14th and 15th IR) would be organised only in time of war, perhaps the 13th IR was the only one created, and then only in 1932.

7   Articles 2, 8 and 21 of Decree 15,235 of 31 December 1921, and Article 2 of Decree 21,682 of 30 July 1932. Daróz, p. 111. Some sources state that the mounted infantry battalions were finally created during the war, on 30 July 1932, numbered 1st to 3rd, identical to the cavalry divisions. Nevertheless, the author hasn't identified any of them participating in the conflict. Also, it was decreed that the headquarters of 3rd Cavalry Division would not be formed, but perhaps with the outbreak of the war this unit was created and as Daróz mentions it, it is likely to be so.
8   Articles 2 and 21 of Decree 15,235 of 31 December 1921. Despite being mentioned in the regulations, it was also stated that the 6th BE was not going to be activated. However, as it is mentioned during the conflict it probably was activated and recruited during the war.
9   Articles 7, 8, 9 and 21 of Decree 15,235 of 31 December 1921. Decree 21,106 of 29 February 1932.
10 Peres Zanetti, p. 171. Jowett, pp. 20, 23. Walsh, p. 6. According to Jowett, it consisted of 34,700 infantry, 10,750 cavalry, 8,700 artillery and 4,300 military police. Perhaps in the latter figure this author has erroneously included the Federal District FP, who were not regular but State troops, as he later talks about 53,000 regular ones, a number also stated by Walsh, based on the US Embassy Military Attaché reports.
11 Annex, Decree 15,235 of 31 December 1921.
12 Daróz, p. 110, for 1st and 4th Division. Peres Zanetti, p. 152, for 2nd Division. Using data provided by these sources, the author prepared several estimates for the number of troops on either side – based on the units involved. The result was very similar to that cited in official reports. Correspondingly, on average, there were 500 troops assigned to every infantry battalion, and 500 assigned to every *Caçadores*, marine, engineers and cavalry regiment; 1,500 men per infantry regiment; 500 per artillery regiment; 200 for each artillery group; and 100 for each battery, company or cavalry squadron. Also, when there is evidence that some units had lower strength, this author has used the lower figures. For example, for 4th Division at the beginning of the war, or the Paulistas battalions of volunteers, the figure has been reduced to 300 soldiers, sometimes even down to 200. As we will see throughout the text, this was their actual total.
13 McCann, p. 224.
14 Jowett, pp. 20, 23.
15 Peres Zanetti, p. 152.
16 McCann, p. 224.
17 Hilton, pp. 171–74. Cotta, pp. 2, 5, 9. Maranhão, p. 3, for the 27th Provisional Corps.
18 Hilton, pp. 171–76.
19 Ibid.
20 Hilton, pp. 246–48, 255–72, 276, 292. García de Gabiola, p. 66.
21 Donato, pp. 200–02. García de Gabiola, p. 66.
22 For the contributions of the states, see Hilton pp. 159, 171–76. For a total of 100,000 Federals, see Hilton, p. 177, and García Gabiola, p. 66. For more exaggerated and implausible figures, see Donato, p. 126, and Peres and Zanetti, p. 152. By comparison, Walsh (p. 8) quotes about 80,000 combatants in the Federal Army.
23 Walsh, p. 13, quotes about 40 such battalions with up to 24,000–25,000 troops. The latter might be valid for the number of the men actually deployed on the front lines.
24 Ibid.
25 Peres Zanetti, p. 152. García de Gabiola, pp. 64–65. According to Hilton, figures should have been much higher. Correspondingly, the Paulista forces should have included 7,000 troops from Army units, 12,000 reservists and nearly 8,000 FPs. Similarly, he quotes the availability of 8,000 rifles from FP stocks, even if adding that more than 60 percent of these jammed after firing only three shots.
26 Hilton, pp. 104–06, 107–08, and García de Gabiola, pp. 64–65. According to the governmental sources, there should have been 18,500 rifles in the armouries of the 2nd Military Region. However, according to Carvalho Abreu, Director of the War Material Division of the Constitutionalist Army, the actual figure was 29,000, of which 5,000 had not been

calibrated.

27 Hilton, pp. 107, 168. Donato, pp. 187, 189. Ribeiro, pp. 6, 21. Garcia Gabiola, pp. 65–66.

28 Donato, pp. 194–96. Ribeiro, pp. 16–17. The female Paulistas went as far as to draw propaganda posters showing 3 or 4-year-old children wearing uniform, and the slogan, 'If necessary, we will go, too!'

29 Jowett, pp. 23, 33, 45–46. Helio Lopes, p. 13. For the characteristics of weapons, see Cotta, pp. 3, 6.

30 Jowett, pp. 23, 33, 45–46. See Cotta, pp. 3–4, for the characteristics of the Hotchkiss, and in general for the Madsen, Colt, Maxim and ZB guns.

31 www.bulgarianartillery.it

32 Fidelis Soares, p. 5.

33 Hilton, pp. 107–08. See Jowett, pp. 33 and 23, for the 25 Paulista and 150 Federal guns. See Maranhão for the 24 cannons vs 100 Federals. Walsh, pp. 6, 14. As so often when it comes to this war, diverse sources provide very different figures for the number of available guns – especially those operated by the Paulistas. For example, the Vargas government assessed their number as only 22; according to São Paulo's Director Abreu there were more than 50, while Walsh cited 30–36.

34 Jowett, p. 20. Jowett also erroneously cites CV 33/35 tankettes, something not mentioned by any other source. Cotta, pp. 2, 5, 9.

35 Della Rosa. Jowett, p. 33. Ribeiro, 'A Revolução Constitucionalista 1932', *Jornal o Rebate*, p. 24, Daróz III, and Donato, p. 186, for the train weapons.

36 Maranhão, p. 4.

37 Jowett, p. 46.

38 Paraná do Brasil, p. 91.

Chapter 3

1 Daróz, pp. 29–32.

2 Daróz, pp. 48–49. Daróz II, p. 1. Hilton, pp. 211–12.

3 Daróz, pp. 48–59.

4 It is possible that the other three Potez 25 TOEs mentioned, for example, by Hagedorn as still extant in late 1932, were still in the official inventory, but had actually been damaged at an earlier point in time and were then used as a source of spares.

5 Hilton, pp. 193–94, for the Aranha da Silva report. Lintz Geraldo, p. 1. Daróz, pp. 69–71, mentions 10 Potezs. Sandro Peres Zanetti, p. 148, mentions 12 observation and bombardment aircraft that may be Potezs. www.rudnei.cunha.nom.br also cites 12 aircraft. On the other hand, the online LAAHS (Latin American Aviation Historical Society) mentions nine Potezs. Hagedorn (Ch. 12, p. 4) does not provide any figures, although mentioning nine aircraft identified (A-111, 114, 115, 117, 119, 211, 214, 216 and 217). The author of this book has only been able to identify six in combat, a figure that coincides with Aranha da Silva's official report. In late 1932, after the war, Hagedorn speaks of nine Potezs available, so it seems that there were only six operational at the beginning of the war, while the other three (A-111, A-119 and A-214) existed but were useless. As there were also two Paulista Potezs that were destroyed during the war, the final figure agrees with the nine Potezs mentioned by Hagedorn. Also, a Federal aircraft made a forced landing after being 'shot down', but as we have seen, as there were nine aircraft at the end of the war, it seems that it was repaired and not totally destroyed. On top of that, this aircraft is mentioned later in operations. See Daróz, pp. 78, 82, for the machine specifications.

6 Daróz, p. 56.

7 Hagedorn, Ch. 12, pp. 9–10, wrongly states that three Wacos were with the Paulistas, while the fourth may have been brought in by a defector – though without mentioning their registrations. Lintz Geraldo Moreira Bento says there were only two at the beginning, but he wrongly included in that number the one brought to the Paulistas by the defector. The only author that clarifies these facts properly is Daróz, pp. 72, 117, citing the registration numbers of all three Wacos operated by the Paulistas (although later, by mistake, mentioning also the C-2 as operated by the Federals).

8 Daróz, pp. 118, 237. Hagedorn Ch 12, pp. 12, 13. See also Della Rosa Web, visited in 2015.

9 Hagedorn, p. 176.

10 Hagedorn, Ch 12, p. 12. See Daróz, pp. 79–80, 82 for the machine specifications. Notably, according to Daróz (p. 79), there should have been no such problems with any newly acquired Waco C-90s, or their sub-variant Waco Military (also Waco M): these should have been armed in the factory, and the ammunition of correct calibre. Furthermore, these had more powerful engines. Less clear is whether the Air Force acquired only 10 Waco C-90/Ms or – as described further below – up to 15.

Furthermore, Hagedorn, Ch. 12, p. 13, mentions a separate aircraft that arrived around 19 August with another five Wacos CSO, but the Federal Wacos came in groups of five, so this sixth 240A Waco probably refers to the M that existed since before the war. See also Daróz, p. 79.

11 Daróz, pp. 69, 81–82. Sandro Peres Zanetti, p. 148, incorrectly cites only one Nid.72, and the online Latin American Aviation Historical Society does the same. Lintz Geraldo, p. 1, quotes two, as do Daróz (first only one, but he then corrects and mentions two), Aranha da Silva (cited by Hilton, pp. 193–94), and Hagedorn, Ch. 12, p. 4.

12 Daróz, p. 69, claimed only one Amiot. Aranha (cited by Hilton, pp. 193–94) is unclear whether there was one or two. Lintz Geraldo, p. 1, said that there were two, as does the online Latin American Aviation Historical Society (LAAHS). Zanetti, p. 148, seems to suggest one. www.rudnei.cunha.nom.br also states one. Hagedorn, Ch. 12, p. 4, mentions that two remained active at the end of 1932 after the war, with plates 621 K and K-624, and that the two Amiots fought, but there are no details or sources mentioned.

13 Hagedorn, Ch. 12, p. 4, mentions three 'Loire' instead of Lioré. Daróz does not mention them. Sandro Peres Zanetti, p. 148, is unclear whether he is talking of the Lioré or the Amiot. Lintz Geraldo, p. 1, is not clear whether it refers to one or two Lioré, as is Director of the Air Service, cited by Hilton, pp. 193–94. Characteristics of the Lioré in www.revolvy.com, visited on 14 September 2018.

14 Daróz, pp. 69–71, 81–82, 138; Hagedorn, Ch. 12, pp. 6, 21; Sandro Peres Zanetti, p. 148; www.rudnei.cunha.nom.br. All these authors agree on 11 Moths. However, Hagedorn mentions the plates of only six known as serving in the war. The Latin American Aviation Historical Society (LAAHS) speaks of only four DH-60 Moths.

15 Hagedorn, Ch 12, pp. 3–5.

16 Daróz, pp. 71, 73, mentions 12 Navy Moths, but only identifies the plates of six of them as serving, p. 138. Peres Zanetti, p. 148, also seems to refer to 12 Navy Moths when he talks about 14 reconnaissance aircraft (perhaps 12 Moths and two Avros). Hagedorn, Ch. 12, p. 6, speaks of nine Navy Moths surviving at the end of the war. However, Hagedorn wrongly collected the plates of only three of them as known to have served in the war. Also, on the online Latin American Aviation Historical Society (LAAHS) and www.rudnei.cunha.nom.br only three of them are mentioned. For how they were armed, see Daróz, p. 138, and Hagedorn, Ch 12, p. 21.

17 Hagedorn, pictorial book, p. 80, see picture note top right.

18 Daróz, pp. 71, 88–89, mentions two Avros, as does www.rudnei.cunha.nom.br. Hagedorn, Ch 12, p. 7, mentions the plates of six Avros bought by Brazil before the war, with numbers 441 to 446, of which at year's end none were available.

19 Daróz, pp. 71, 82–83. Hagedorn Ch 12, p. 6, informs us that there were five SM.55s active once the war had finished. Also, only three Martins and seven SM.55s appear on the online Latin American Aviation Historical Society (LAAHS), in www.rudnei.cunha.nom.br, and it could also be deduced from the ten aircraft (perhaps seven SM.55 and three Martins) mentioned by Zanetti, p. 148.

20 Daróz, pp. 71, 85. Hagedorn Ch 12, p. 6, informs us that only two Martins remained once the war had finished at the end of 1932.

21 Some sources cite them as operated by the '18th Observation Division', which never actually existed.

22 Daróz, pp. 70, 85, 86. www.rudnei.cunha.nom.br and Sandro Peres Zanetti, p. 148, for the 18th Naval Division. Also, four Corsairs are mentioned in Daróz, Hagedorn, Ch 12, p. 6, Lintz Geraldo, p. 1, Peres Zanetti and Aranha da Silva (cited by Hilton, pp. 193–94).

23 Daróz, pp. 91, 96. See Della Rosa, Lintz Geraldo, p. 4, and Moreira Bento, p.10, for the incident involving the Taguató (the name of the aircraft is not mentioned by Moreira nor Lintz). See Flores Jr, p. 459, for the names of the four aircraft. Hagedorn, p. 26, mentions only the Kyri-Kyri and wrongly the Kanuiré-Y. Walsh, p. 14, also mentions 10 aircraft, with only four able to undertake any combat missions.

24 Hagedorn, pp. 30–31. A comparison of contemporary photographs is problematic because only black and white photographs are available and because it is possible that sometimes a light blue colour was used instead of blue.

25 Daroz, pp. 237–46.

Chapter 4

1 Donato, pp. 77–82.

2 Daróz, pp. 117–18, 237, is the only source that correctly mentions Wacos C-2 and C-5. Moreira Bento, p. 9, erroneously cited C-2 and C-3.

Hagedorn, Ch 12, p. 9, however, mentions three Wacos at the beginning, and then added one more defecting.

3 Hilton, p. 85. Silva, p. 205.

4 Daróz, p. 117.

5 Hilton, p. 194.

6 Daróz, p. 72. Hagedorn, Ch 12, p. 9, also mentions two DH-60 Moths, instead of three, and added the Fleet, the Ni-80, two Ni-81s, the Monocoupé, the Breda, the Avro, the S.56 and two Caudrons to Daróz's list. Hagedorn also mentions the owner of each aircraft. Lintz Geraldo, p. 4, mistakenly mentions only Waco C-2, and then later a second Waco that defected to the Paulistas. This author also mentions a single DH-60 Moth rather than three of them, and he adds a Fleet not mentioned by Daróz despite later stating that a Fleet crashed when it was transporting General Klinger.

7 Hagedorn, Ch 12, pp. 12–13.

8 Donato, pp. 74–86. Hilton, pp. 84–87.

9 Donato, p. 88. (Also the source of the title of this section).

10 Hilton, p. 87. Silva, pp. 206–09. Ramos, p. 11.

11 Donato, pp. 76, 88. The author is not aware of any Heavy Artillery Regiment, only of Independent Groups. Also, Donato mentions 08:00hrs on 10 July, while Monteiro reacted on the previous day, 9 July, at 18:00hrs (Ramos, p. 7, and Hilton, p. 83).

12 Hilton, pp. 92–95. Ramos, p. 7. Garcia Gabiola, p. 64.

13 Ramos, p. 7. Hilton, p. 97.

14 Coutinho, p. 196.

15 Of the listed BCs, the author was unable to reconstruct the operations of the 24th, 26th, and 28th. Probably garrisoning Maranhao, the 24th seems to have been redeployed into Mato Grosso do Sul; the 26th probably remained in Pará, while the 28th stood in Sergipe.

16 Hilton, pp. 79, 98–99.

17 Donato, p. 100.

18 Coutinho, p. 196. In one of his earlier publications, the author wrongly stated (based on Daróz, p. 111) that the three cavalry divisions served in the south. However, a cross-examination of reports by all the independent cavalry regiments has revealed that all the cavalry units serving there (namely the 9th, 12th and 14th RCI) were almost exclusively from 3rd Cavalry Division. Only 1st RCI of 1st Cavalry Division and 5th RCI from 2nd Cavalry Division were deployed on the same, southern, front line (the latter to occupy Mato Grosso do Sul, but not Paraná). On the contrary, it seems that the balance of 1st and 2nd Cavalry Divisions remained deployed in Rio Grande do Sul, to protect the border with Argentina and Uruguay, and thus spent most of the war without actively participating in combat operations. Meanwhile, the entire 3rd Infantry Division was deployed on the southern front, with the exception of its 9th RI, 3rd RCD and 3rd BE: the former was redeployed to the Paraíba Valley in the east and then to Minas Gerais, while 3rd RCD and 3rd BE were redeployed to Mato Grosso do Sul. Summarizing, most of 3rd Cavalry Division and elements of 1st and 2nd Cavalry Divisions were redeployed to strengthen 5th Military Region (and thus 5th Infantry Division), when this led the final offensive on São Paulo. Regarding 5th Division, the 14th and 15th RI, the 10th RAM, and the 5th BE, that is, half of the unit, did not fight in this sector and were probably left garrisoning Paraná.

19 Donato, pp. 94–95.

20 Daróz, p. 119. Daróz (p. 73) first claimed one Amiot, the registration of which is known, and then two. Hilton (pp. 193–94), quoting Aranha, the Director of Aviation, also mentioned one Amiot but also a Lioré et Olivier Leo-253Bn.4: this is the probable source of Daróz's confusion. Nevertheless, the Leo-253 should not be listed as operational because, as explained by Hagedorn (p. 77), this aircraft was never used due to the lack of a crew qualified to fly it. Moreover, Hilton, (pp. 193–94), cites a Memorandum from Aviation Director Mr Aranha da Silva, in which the availability of six Potezs is mentioned. This matches the registration numbers cross-examined by the author. However, other authors – mistakenly – quote up to 10 such aircraft (for example, Daróz, pp. 69–71), or even 12 (for example, Lintz Geraldo, p. 1). Finally, Hagedorn (Ch. 12, p.4) listed nine Potezs, including A-111, A-119 and A-214.

21 Several authors cite 11 Moths (Peres Zanetti, p. 148, generically as 11 liaison aircraft in the Military School, or Daróz, pp. 69–71), but Hagedorn, Ch. 12, p. 6, has identified only six Moth plates in the conflict.

22 Hilton, pp. 87–89. According to Daróz, the aircraft actually suffered damage on landing in Avaré. Hilton, p. 88, mentions Baurú. Daróz pp. 118, 237, states it was a Fleet, but speaks of Avaré.

23 Hagedorn, Ch 12, p. 16.

24 Daróz, pp. 119–20. Lintz Geraldo, p. 5, about the escorting Corsair. Hagedorn, p. 16.

25 Daróz, p. 246.

26 Daróz, pp. 119–20, mentions that Wacos C-1, C-2 and C-3 were equipped with Federal arms. As it is known that C-2 was held by the rebels, the author believes that he actually refers to C-1, C-3 and C-4.

27 Daróz, pp. 122, 123, 237. Hagedorn, Ch 12, p. 17. Geraldo Lintz, p. 5.

28 Hilton, pp. 193, 201–02, 204–05, 214–15. Lintz Geraldo, p. 5. Daróz, pp. 122, 216.

29 Daróz, pp. 123–24. Other authors erroneously date this action as being on 15 July or even 21 July, such as Moreira Bento, p. 9. Hagedorn, Ch 12, pp. 17, 18, does not even mention the defection, assuming that Waco C-3 was with the rebels from the beginning.

Chapter 5

1 Figure mentioned in Daróz, p. 110.

2 Entire Federal deployment in Ramos, p. 8, completed by Hilton, p. 129. The estimation, made by the author, is based on 1,500 men per infantry regiment, 1,000 per artillery regiment with 24 pieces, and 500 troopers per cavalry battalion or regiment. Adding three infantry regiments, two artillery regiments, one cavalry regiment, one engineer battalion and three light infantry battalions, it gives a total of 9,000 soldiers composing the entire division, closely matching the 9,061 men officially present on 16 July.

3 Hilton, p. 112.

4 Silva. pp. 209–10. For the composition of each detachment, and the segregation between the Detachments Abilio and Abreu, see Ramos, Annex B, pp. A III, A IV, dated 20 July. The calculation of effective soldiers is an estimate by the author of this book, about 500 soldiers per regular battalion, 300 per volunteer battalion, 100 per company or squadron and 50 per artillery battery.

5 Ramos, Annex B, p. A III.

6 Daróz, pp. 125–26, 246.

7 Daróz, p. 126.

8 Hilton, p. 195, states that the Paulista air operations started later and on the southern front, against Paraná.

9 Lintz Geraldo, p. 3. The Paulistas were not the only ones to stage spectacular defections. The Federalist pilot Geraldo Aquino, who was in São Paulo at the time of the revolt, refused to serve with the rebels, and was jailed. However, he managed to flee and reach Rio de Janeiro, on 15 July, where he joined the Federal Aviation in Resende.

10 Daróz, pp. 124, 126–28. Hilton, p. 194. Lintz Geraldo, p. 3.

11 Daróz, p. 237. Hagedorn, Ch 12, pp. 12–13.

12 Hagedorn, Ch. 12, p.12.

13 No author cites the plate of the Waco but taking into account that the C-3 had defected and Waco 'M' was damaged it could only be one of the two remaining in service: C-1 or the C-4.

14 Daróz, p. 128. Hagedorn, Ch 12, p. 17, differs slightly from Daróz when he says that two Wacos departed from Resende to drop pamphlets on São Paulo, and another two Potezs and a Corsair bombed the Campo de Marte. According to him, the next day three Potezs, one Amiot, and two Wacos returned to bomb Campo de Marte again, while another solitary Potez attacked Taubaté. We are not sure whether Hagedorn or Daróz confused the dates. Perhaps there were attacks both on both the 16th and 17th. On the other hand, according to Daróz, the new airfield in Resende was not operational until the second half of August, so the government squadron could hardly have departed from there. Lintz Geraldo, p. 5, says that there were three Potezs and one Amiot that bombed the Campo de Marte, while one Waco dropped propaganda, escorted by another Waco and a Corsair. Hilton, pp. 200, 212–17, mentions 17 July.

15 Daróz, pp. 128–29, states that it was in the second half of August, but Moreira Bento, p. 3, states specifically that the airport was operational on 27 July, which seems more reasonable: 13 days of work instead of 43. However, according to Hagedorn, Chap. 12, p. 16, the aerodrome was operational at least from 16 July, which seems too early, in addition to contradicting the two Brazilian authors.

16 Silva, p. 211, and Ramos, p. 9. According Hilton, p. 130, the first clash was on 14 July.

17 Hagedorn, Ch 12, p. 17. Hilton, pp. 200, 212, 217, seems to confirm an attack on 17 July, although the former says that it was made by three Potezs, an Amiot and two Wacos that were returning after bombing Campo de Marte, while another solitary Potez was attacking Taubaté. These numbers are suspiciously similar to the attack made on 16 July. On the other hand, to add more confusion, Hilton says that this attack with

four aircraft was the largest of the war until then, thereby obviating the six airframes that according Daróz were launched on 16 July.

18 Daróz, p. 131, does not identify the plates of the Wacos, but as there were only three serviceable in the Federal forces there is no doubt which ones they were. Hagedorn, Ch.12, pp.19–20, also agrees on the importance of the bombing but, contradicting himself, quotes them as departing from Dos Afonsos instead of Resende. For Góis' plan, see Hilton, pp. 205–06; also for Montezuma, on p. 207, and for the train, on p. 212.

19 Silva, p. 211. Silva claims that they were the equivalent of a single Paulista battalion versus two Federal battalions and had deployed in defensive positions. If these government units were at full strength, as he claims, and we take the nine Paulista units as being company-sized, there would be some 900 Paulistas against 2,000 government troops (three infantry battalions and a cavalry regiment). Despite this, according Donato (p. 144), Santana was occupied by the rebels, but they were later forced to evacuate it. Silva says that it was the Federal 1st RI, however the 2nd was part of the Detachment Fontoura, and the 1st was located further north, so is likely to be a mistake.

20 Daróz, p. 132. Hilton, pp.195, 201–02. Lintz Geraldo, p. 6.

21 Daróz, pp. 133–36, 251. Donato, pp. 137, 144. See Hilton, p. 200, about Góis. On p. 218 Hilton contradicts and exaggeratedly claims there were 15 airframes escorted by three Corsairs. Lintz Geraldo, p. 6.

22 Moreira Bento, p. 4.

23 Moreira Bento, p. 3 (he stated that they moved 'eighteen days after the beginning of the revolution') and p. 7. The author claims that this Potez was carrying three crew, as besides the pilot he mentions Lieutenants Aquino and Anizio. Perhaps this aircraft was an Amiot and not a Potez.

24 Silva, pp. 211–12. Donato, p. 144. Hilton, pp. 129, 136, 206.

25 Hilton, p. 200. Daróz, p. 238.

26 Ramos, Annex B, p. A IV.

27 Silva, pp. 212–14.

28 Ibid.

29 Donato, p. 144.

30 Ramos, p. 9. Silva, p. 213. Hilton, p. 135.

31 Hilton, pp. 121, 208.

32 Donato, p. 142. Donato dates these operations 15–28 August, but this must be a mistake and perhaps should be changed to July, when Ramos mentioned this operation; the Fazenda Palmeira is slightly south of Salto, and therefore in August this place was far behind the Federal lines.

33 Ramos, p. 9. Silva, p. 214. Hilton, pp. 136–37.

34 Silva, pp. 214–16.

35 Donato, p. 144.

36 Donato, p. 139. This author also cites Federal aviation, but we have no record by other authors of airstrikes, due to bad weather.

37 Silva, pp. 216–17.

38 Daróz, pp. 141–42. Hagedorn, Ch. 12, p. 22. Hilton, pp. 203, 208, 212.

39 Moreira Bento, p. 6, and Hilton, p. 208.

40 Silva, pp. 217–18. Hilton, p. 138.

41 Ramos, pp. 19, 20, and Donato, p. 136.

42 Ramos, p. 19.

43 Silva, p. 219.

44 Ramos, p. 19.

45 Silva, pp. 219–22. For the blowing of the bridge by Bresser, see Donato, p. 142. Hilton, p. 138.

46 Daróz, pp. 136–45.

47 Hagedorn, Ch. 12, and Daróz, pp. 23, 145. Hilton, pp. 211, 219.

48 Donato, p. 145.

49 Daróz, p. 146, Hagedorn, Ch. 12, p. 23.

50 Daróz, pp. 146, 213. Hilton, p. 215. Donato, p. 142. Hagedorn, Ch. 12, pp. 23–24, says that it was on 14 August, and that there were five aircraft. Regarding the date, it must be wrong, because the Federal Potezs bombed the power plant on the 13th, when this incident took place. However, Daróz first says it was the 13th, and then the 12th, so the date is not clear.

51 Moreira Bento, p. 4.

52 Hagedorn, Ch. 12, pp. 23–24. Hilton, p. 219. Daróz, pp. 146–47. Moreira Bento, p. 5.

53 Daróz, pp. 147, 151, and Moreira Bento, p. 5, both say that these aircraft moved to Campo de Marte, although Moreira seems to state that they departed earlier, on the 14th. Hagedorn, Ch. 12, pp. 23–24, says that they moved to the south. Maybe they stopped in São Paulo before heading to the south. Hilton, p. 219. According to Daróz, the attacks were unsuccessful because the Paulista aviation had departed the same day.

54 Silva, pp. 222–25.

55 Donato, pp. 140–42.

56 Daróz, p. 147. Hilton, pp. 206, 208, and Moreira Bento, p. 6

57 Daróz, p. 149. Hilton, p. 220. Lintz Geraldo, p. 3, states that these actions were made on the 21st, but Hagedorn, Ch. 12, p. 24, says that Murici's flight was the day after the defection; this is wrong, because Hilton cites Murici's report that is dated the 20th. For Moreira Bento, p. 9, the defector was NiD K-421.

58 Daróz, p. 149.

59 Hilton, pp. 212–20. This order was issued on 22 August. Hilton mentioned that several missions were made following these instructions, expressly on at least 23, 26 and 27 September.

60 Lintz Geraldo, p. 6; Donato, p. 147; Hagerdon, Ch. 12, p. 24; Daróz, pp. 150–51, 217; and Moreira Bento, p. 5, agreed that the Paulistas had two aircraft, but Daróz includes the story in São Paulo's newspaper La Gazeta, which mentions three aircraft and three rebel pilots. The NiD.72 K-422, the third Federal aircraft, is not mentioned by Lintz, Donato, or Moreira, but is mentioned by Daróz in II (¿Aviação de caza e pesca?), pp. 255–56, explains that this NiD was in the rear, far from the fighting area, which was the reason why it did not fight, and perhaps this is also the reason for it being ignored by the other authors. For the names of the Federal pilots, see Moreira Bento. Regarding the date, all authors agree that this combat was on 22 August. Consequently, the 22nd should appear in the report of the Mixed Group, cited by Daróz II, but surprisingly the date of 21st is also used by Daróz I, in the Gazeta, contradicting himself. Perhaps the report was made a day after the clash.

61 Potez A-114 is cited as moving to the south on 5 or 11 August by Daróz and Hagedorn, so it is not clear that this plate number data is correct, unless it had returned to Paraíba.

62 Daróz, p. 151. Hagedorn, Ch. 12, p. 24, this time coincides with the date, and mentions three government Potezs and two Wacos, and describes the Paulistas aircraft parked on the road. Donato, p. 140, and Lintz Geraldo, p. 6, also agree with the date and the result.

63 Daróz, pp. 151–52, identifies the surprised aircraft on the ground as a Paulista CurtissO-1E Falcon, but this seems impossible, since the Falcon would not arrive until 1 or 3 September.

64 Hagedorn, Ch. 12, p. 25.

65 Moreira Bento, p. 6.

66 Daróz, pp. 151–52, 155.

67 Ramos, p. 20.

68 Daróz, p. 152.

69 Donato, p. 140.

70 Ramos, p. 20.

71 Silva, pp. 225–28.

72 Moreira Bento, p.6. Daróz, p. 153.

73 Ramos, p. 20.

74 Daróz, p. 155. Donato, p. 147, mentions vermelinho airstrikes, of which there is also evidence in Hilton, pp. 208, 212.

75 Silva, pp. 225–28.

76 Ramos, p. 20.

77 Donato, p. 145.

78 Ramos, Annex B, p. A III.

79 Ramos, Map 4, p. 16.

80 The contribution of 10th RI is described as a battery but was probably a battalion.

81 Cotta. As Trincheiras da Mantiqueira, pp. 1–5, 7. Note that the figures given are as per the original source and that the total does not correspond with the individual figures. It is not clear which figures are correct.

82 Donato, p. 142.

83 Silva, p. 208.

84 Donato, p. 147.

85 Donato, pp. 129, 140.

86 Ramos, p. 14.

87 Cotta, p. 6.

88 Silva, pp. 229–30.

89 Donato states the 12th.

90 Donato, pp. 142, 145.

91 Silva, pp. 229–30. Donato, pp. 136, 142.

92 Donato, p. 136.

93 Hilton, p. 142.

94 Silva, pp. 231–32.

95 Silva, p. 232.

96 Silva, p. 232.

97 Silva, p. 232.

98 Hilton, p. 108, contains the figure of 20,000 Paulista soldiers, a figure collected from Figueiredo. García de Gabiola, p. 66, also accepted this figure in a previous work, but now it seems doubtful, since 20,000 troops was, as we shall see, the strength of the Federals in the Paraíba, and as we have been seeing and we will see later in detail, these had a large numerical superiority. Also, Maranhão, p. 3, speaks of 10,000 Paulistas against 20,000 Federals.

99 Hilton, p. 143.

100 Hilton, p. 121.

101 Lourival Cotinho, p. 211, that catches the words of Góis Monteiro.

102 Moreira Bento, p. 6, cites three Wacos piloted by Araripe (the Group Commander) and Lieutenants Julio and Nero Moura. Daróz, p. 155, does not provide a date of arrival but states that it took four days to assemble them. Moreira Bento, p. 6, states that they were operating on 8 September. Remaining details from Daróz, p. 155.

103 Hilton, pp. 208, 204–05, 206, 208.

104 Hagedorn, Ch. 12, p. 26, states that the freighter arrived on 9 September.

105 Daróz, pp. 160, 164, and Moreira Bento, p. 7. Lintz Geraldo, p. 4. While many sources cite additional deliveries at subsequent points in time, the author could not find any evidence for further aircraft acquisitions.

106 This will be covered in Volume 2.

107 Lintz Geraldo, p. 7.

108 Daróz, p. 231.

109 Silva, pp. 233–35.

110 Ramos, p. 10. Hilton, p. 143.

111 Silva, p. 235.

112 Hilton, p. 144.

113 Donato, p. 145.

114 Silva, pp. 235–36.

115 Cotta, p. 9.

116 Ramos, p. 10.

117 Hilton, p. 207.

118 Ramos, p. 21, Annex C. Hilton, p. 144.

119 Moreira Bento, p. 7.

120 Ramos, p. 10, and Hilton, pp. 143–44.

121 Moreira Bento, p. 7. Instead, Daróz, p. 164, suggests that bad weather deprived air support to the Federals between 13 and 16 September. It seems that that the interventions cited by Moreira are correct, so perhaps it should be understood that they performed not massive actions, but several by isolated aircraft or pairs of aircraft, as Daróz attests happened on 15 September.

122 Ramos, pp. 10, 21, Annex C.

123 Daróz, p. 164.

124 Silva, pp. 237–41.

125 Cotta, p. 9.

126 Ramos, p. 21.

127 Or the Detachment Teófilo, according to Donato, p. 138. Ramos, p. 21, speaks of the Teófilo Detachment being defeated by the Federals, as it was not helped by the Detachment Andrade. For the weapons and name of the train, see Della Rosa, p. 2.

128 Silva, pp. 241–42.

129 Silva, p. 241. Donato, p. 138.

130 Daróz, p. 168 and Moreira Bento, p. 7, surprisingly speaks of two Paulista Falcons captured in Cruzeiro that were moved to Resende on 11 September to take part in a parade for the civilians see, which is not mentioned by any other author. Perhaps it should be read as 11 October, after the Paulista surrender, when the Federals had captured all of the Paulista Falcons.

131 Daróz, II, p. 168, and Moreira Bento, p. 7.

132 Hagedorn, Ch 12, p. 26, mistakenly says this leaflet mission was on 9 September, and also that the enemy aircraft attacking the Paulistas were three Wacos, rather than two Wacos and one Potez.

133 Hagedorn, Ch 12, p. 26, and Daróz, pp. 164–65.

134 Lintz Geraldo, p. 7. This author also claims that Lysias's gunner, Machado Bittencourt, shot down an aircraft, a fact that is repeated by Donato, p. 128, but this is simply based on the testimony of soldiers who saw the combat from the ground and claimed to see a smoking aircraft dive down. Donato also confuses the date for the fight over Cruzeiro, saying it took place on 24 September.

135 Ramos, Annex D, pp. A VI and VII A, and Ramos, p. 22, where the *Bombardas* Companies are called Fire Brigade companies. Silva cites a slightly different display here, but we trust more at this point to Ramos. Silva, p. 242, states that the Gaia Detachment was organised on the left

136 bank of the Paraíba, with Teófilo to the right of the river and the railroad, and Sampaio from the railroad to the Quebra Cangalha ridges.

136 Helio Lopes, p. 6, provides the data on the military units involved. The calculation of the troops has been made by the author of this work, at the rate of 1,500 soldiers per infantry regiment, 500 per battalion, 1,000 per artillery regiment (or 500 for part of a regiment), about 100 per artillery or infantry group, some 1,000 for Detachment Cunha and about 500 for elements or remains of a detachment or regiment.

137 Lourival Coutinho, p. 211, for the fifth Detachment Ferreira. Góis mentions in this work 40,000 Federal soldiers in 10 detachments, with half in Paraíba. Hilton, p. 131, gives the figure of 34,000 soldiers. García de Gabiola, p. 66, in a previous article assumed wrongly this last figure was only for the Paraíba, but it was for both this theatre and the Minas front. Maranhão, p. 3, also states 20,000 Federals in the Paraíba.

138 Daróz, pp. 241, 211.

139 Moreira Bento, p. 7. Here Moreira erroneously states that a Paulista Potez was destroyed, a difficult thing to accomplish when all the rebel aviation was deployed in Campinas, facing the Minas sector, and both existing Potezs had already been destroyed. Perhaps he confused this loss with the one on 21 September in Minas.

140 Moreira Bento, pp.7–8. The accident of the first Moth is also quoted on the web at Desastresaereos.net, but is probably wrong when it fixes the date one month earlier, on 27 August, and also confuses the crash site, placing it in the Itaguaí ridges. We know that in this last place Moth 3003 crashed. Moreira Bento and Daróz, pp. 175–76, state that a Moth with plate number K-150 crashed on 27 September. Perhaps the website could refer also to an earlier accident at the same spot, since the plate mentioned is K-130 instead of the K-150 mentioned in other sources.

141 Moreira Bento, p. 8

142 Daróz, p. 237.

143 Silva, pp. 242, 249.

144 Lourival Cotinho, p. 211.

145 Ramos, pp. 10, 21.

Chapter 6

1 Ramos, p. 58.

2 Ramos, p. 17, Map 5.

3 Hilton, p. 255.

4 Daróz, pp. 89, 93.

5 Daróz, pp. 120–21. Hagedorn, Ch 12, p. 21.

6 Daróz says that they were six Savoias, but this seems wrong, because at this time only three had been deployed in Ilhabela.

7 Daróz, p. 122 and Hilton, p. 202.

8 Daróz, p. 126.

9 Silva, pp. 242–243. Calculations made by the current author, at a rate of 100 soldiers per company and 30 per section.

10 Silva, pp. 243, 245, Ramos, p. 52. Donato, p. 138. This author believes that due to the low rank of the commander, a mere captain, it is likely that Ramos and Donato were right. Instead, the three battalions cited by Silva could refer to a later time, when the detachment was reinforced.

11 Hilton, p. 113.

12 Hilton, p. 202. Reports from the observer Perdigão.

13 Daróz, p. 130; Hagedorn, Ch. 12, p. 20. Hilton, p. 211, for the Paulista Waco. According to Hagedorn, the Corsair pilots also saw what seemed to be a Paulista Potez but lost it in the clouds.

14 Daróz, p. 130. Hagedorn, Ch. 12, pp. 20–21, as usual, states the bombing was a couple of days later, on 21 July. While authors such as Daróz and Hagedorn claim that this air strike destroyed the artillery battery that prevented the Federal attack on Cunha, the available Paulista order of battle lists no artillery unit deployed in this combat zone.

15 Silva, pp. 243–45. Ramos, p. 58. Donato, p. 138. Four Paulista companies are mentioned by Donato and Ramos, but Silva disagrees. The detail of the starting position in the Morro are also in Donato and Ramos, who also mention the presence of the poet and the number of prisoners. The remaining details are from Silva.

16 Daróz, p. 132.

17 Daróz, p. 137.

18 Hilton, pp. 214–15.

19 Daróz, p. 137. Hagedorn, Ch 12, p. 21, gives the detail of the escorting Corsair, and places the last bombing on 29 July. Hilton, p. 215, says that there was a single Corsair and two seaplanes on 29 and 30 July.

20 Daróz, pp. 137, 138, mentions a patrol of two aircraft, one with radio and one with machine guns and bombs, contradicting the sections of three aircraft that we have already seen. Meanwhile, Hagedorn, Ch. 12, p. 21,

assigns them a radio, gun and bombs on each aircraft of each section.

21 Hagedorn, Ch. 12, p. 12.
22 Daróz, p. 139.
23 Silva, pp. 246–47. Daróz, p. 147, for the lack of air support due to bad weather. Hilton, p. 113, for the new commander.
24 Silva, p. 248.
25 Daróz, pp. 142, 145, 149. Hagedorn, Ch. 12, p. 23.
26 Hagedorn, Ch. 12, p. 22. The return of the Corsair from Resende to Vila Bela is deduced by this author from the mention made of it by Hagedorn on a mission on 3 September.
27 Daróz, pp. 155–56. Hagedorn, p. 25, agrees.
28 Hagedorn, Ch. 12, p. 26, and Daróz, pp. 163–64.
29 Lintz Geraldo, p. 7.
30 Daróz, pp. 169–70. Hagedorn, Ch. 12, p. 27.
31 This cruiser has been wrongly identified as a battleship by several authors, including the current author in a previous article (Garcia de Gabiola, p. 66)
32 Daróz, pp. 170–71. Hagedorn, Ch. 12, pp. 27, 28. Hilton, pp. 221–22.
33 Daróz, pp. 171–72. Hilton, pp. 221–22.
34 Hagedorn, Ch. 12, p. 20, cites it as a Pan Am, but it seems it was a Brazilian Panair. Daróz, pp. 174–75, seems to suggest that the watchman was also involved. Nevertheless, in such a case, why did the aircraft crash? The press said that this was the action of a Federal fighter.
35 Silva, pp. 248–49.
36 Ramos, pp. 10, 21. Ramos is the only author to mention these movements of the final offensive made by Cavalcanti, but no author has assessed that it implied the encirclement from the south of all the Paulista forces in the Paraíba Valley.

ACKNOWLEDGMENTS

I would like to thank in the first place my Brazilian friends who helped me to carry out this work: André Naves, the first person who talked to me about this war; Luiz Fernando de Mello Camargo, who selflessly sent me the first books I had about this topic directly from Brazil; First Lieutenant Ana Izabel, who provided me with remote access to some of the works placed in the ECEME library; Luiz Eduardo Silva Parreira, who provided me with his unpublished work; and Eric Lucian Apolinário and Carlos Daróz, who delivered or gave me access to their excellent books for free.

But above all, I want to dedicate this work to my mother-in-law, Chitina Zamora, who assisted me to write this book in her wonderful country house in El Puerto, Sierra Espuña, Murcia, during August 2018; and also to my wife, Carolina Martínez Zamora, for encouraging me to complete this work and for her patience, enduring my hours of absence during the holidays.

ABOUT THE AUTHOR

Javier Garcia de Gabiola, from Spain, works as a lawyer and has published numerous articles and books related to legal issues. Always interested in military history, he also regularly contributes to various Spanish military history magazines, for which he has written more than 50 articles. He has also published multiple pieces with the Universidad Autónoma de México. This is his first instalment for Helion's @War series.